Old Sturbridge Village

Old Sturbridge Village

KENT McCALLUM

WITH PHOTOGRAPHS BY THOMAS NEILL

JACK LARKIN, CONSULTING EDITOR

HARRY N. ABRAMS, INC., PUBLISHERS

Editor: Eric Himmel
Editorial Assistant: Rachel Tsutsumi
Designer: Dirk Luykx

Title page: Old Sturbridge Village—the Common in winter

Library of Congress Cataloging-in-Publication Data
McCallum, Kent, 1940–
    Old Sturbridge Village / Kent McCallum ; with photographs by
Thomas Neill ; Jack Larkin, consulting editor.
    p.   cm.
    Includes index.
    ISBN 0-8109-3686-0
    1. Old Sturbridge Village.   2. City and town life—New England—
History—19th century.   I. Title.
F74.S93M44   1996
974.4'3—dc20   96-6909

Published in 1996 by Harry N. Abrams, Incorporated, New York
A Times Mirror Company

Printed and bound in Japan

CONTENTS

PRESIDENT'S MESSAGE

A HALF CENTURY AGO, OLD STURBRIDGE VILLAGE WAS FOUNDED as an experiment in "outdoor history." The results of that experiment are no longer in doubt. Over the course of these five decades the Village has succeeded in reaching millions of visitors with its story of early New England life. It has become a superb model of what is a typically American style of museum: open, dynamic, and engaging. Visitors are encouraged to be participants rather than observers, and history becomes an inviting journey into the past, making learning personal and unforgettable.

Old Sturbridge Village has taken its place not only as a significant regional presence, but also as an important part of the cultural landscape of the nation. One of the three largest outdoor museums in the United States, the Village serves in many ways as a public monument to the American story, both inclusive and powerful.

The American small town found its origin in New England communities like Sturbridge, and in the Village we have created a living stage that plays out daily the drama of responsible citizenship for today's visitors. The museum preserves the legacy of ordinary people who worked, raised families, and built communities. Every day we immerse visitors in the rhythms and values of New England's traditional rural life while also giving them a broader historical perspective.

Unlike most of our encounters with history, Old Sturbridge Village does not immortalize the famous, but rather discloses a new way of seeing the history we have long taken for granted. Here through the everyday settings and stories of small-community residents like blacksmith Emerson Bixby, the widow Fenno, farmer Pliny Freeman, immigrant Mary Culligan, or African-American healer Peter Clark, our visitors can relate past to present, and even present to future.

Every day, costumed "interpreters" demonstrate the work and celebrations of life in rural nineteenth-century New England. This constantly renewed chronicle of everyday history documents a past that might otherwise be forgotten. The re-created wedding of Salem Towne's spirited daughter Sally and her childhood friend Abijah Brown, a re-created funeral for widow Fenno's boarder, the festivities of our Agricultural Fair, all expand the boundaries of museum presentation, moving to what may be thought of as a new kind of American historical theater. They are crucial aspects of the past that can only be hinted at in textbooks and classrooms.

There are lessons for us today as the Village explores the reaction of these men and women of the 1830s to the emerging technology and changing ideas that were transforming their world. Some of the nation's great achievements as well as its everyday textures are evident in the Village's daily and special events. Where else might one find the Declaration of Independence—the rationale that set a new republic on its course over two hundred years ago—celebrated so dramatically by an annual public reading?

As a nation we position education at the foundation of our democracy, a crucial element for all Americans in achieving social, economic, and intellectual opportunity. Old Sturbridge Village, through the creative interaction of its scholarship and its dynamic teaching, provides students of all ages with an encounter with the past—its sights, sounds, smells, tastes, and textures. Although preservation continues to be central to our mission, of even greater importance is the way in which we draw upon our collections and knowledge to give a vitally important dimension of meaning to our nation's history.

Old Sturbridge Village is a very special museum. We invite you to walk the pathways, chat with costumed "villagers," hear the music and learn the dance steps for a Birthnight Ball, join a citizens' parade on Independence Day . . . and imagine what it might have been like to live in a rural New England community in the early years of this republic.

Alberta Sebolt George
President, Old Sturbridge Village

INTRODUCTION

A Great Picture of Society

NO LESS THAN OTHER AMERICANS OF THE 1830s, RURAL NEW
Englanders knew in their bones that they were the children of change. Behind them lay
the traditional world of the eighteenth century, the world of the American Revolution,
of George Washington and John Adams. Many of its features, symbolized even then by
buckled shoes, knee breeches, and powdered wigs, had already disappeared—although
some of the structures of traditional life were enduring and slow to change. A new
world—of factories, railroads, and cities—was starting to take shape before their eyes.
They straddled the divide, living with past and future, tradition and transformation at
the same time.

Set in the rolling hills of central Massachusetts, Old Sturbridge Village, an outdoor museum of early American history, tells their story through the re-creation of everyday life down to its smallest details. Today, a working New England community of the
1830s spreads out across two hundred acres in the town of Sturbridge, the living image
of a past otherwise vanished.

The Village's collections and programs focus on New England in the early years
of the American republic, 1790 to 1840, a time of often wrenching social, economic, and
political change. The museum examines these eventful fifty years from the vantage point
of the ordinary people who made and experienced history. While great events and
notable people will always be extensively chronicled, the Village's purpose is different.
By collecting, preserving, and interpreting commonplace objects and histories, it seeks
to find and present the extraordinary in the ordinary.

"Every individual," wrote one of rural New England's great chroniclers, Harriet
Beecher Stowe, "is part and parcel of a great picture of the society in which he lives
and acts, and his life cannot be painted without reproducing a picture of the world he
lived in."

To provide that picture is the abiding mission of Old Sturbridge Village.
Winding country roads pass through the museum's re-created landscape of plowlands,
hayfields and pastures, rocky woodlots, ponds, and orchards. Carefully restored buildings from all parts of New England, together with a number of painstakingly accurate
reconstructions, are scattered near a crossroads at the millpond and clustered around a
town common. There are working farms, houses, waterpowered mills, meetinghouses,

Opposite: *Resplendent in his officer's uniform, the captain of the militia company prepares to raise a replica of the Continental Army's Grand Union Flag, honoring the veterans of the American Revolution*

artisans' shops, a bank and a law office, a country store and a schoolhouse, along with barns and sheds, privies and fences, gardens and livestock.

Men and women in historical costume—"interpreters" of a past culture—are at work throughout the Village, reenacting for visitors the activities and skills of daily life. They can be found plowing fields and mowing hay, blacksmithing, printing, and tending the mills. They plant gardens, milk cows, cook dinner, press cheese, spin wool, and keep accounts. They manufacture shoes, brooms, lumber, barrels, tinware, pottery, baskets, and bonnets.

They re-create the celebrations and occasions of community life with town meetings, weddings, funerals, Sabbath services, and militia training days. On special occasions, they gather for political speeches, agricultural fairs, and Fourth of July parades. Through song and dance, instrumental music, stories and games, character portrayals and dramatic performances, they evoke the texture of that otherwise nearly forgotten world. In order to help visitors in their individual voyages of exploration, interpreters move easily between the 1830s and the present day. They seek to give visitors not only knowledge but excitement, enjoyment, engagement.

The Village reaches beyond its portrayal of New England community life to provide other perspectives on the material world of the past—a rich diversity of historic objects, many of which can be seen only sparingly in the Village's carefully furnished houses and shops. Gallery displays drawn from the museum's extensive collections explore the history of lighting, New England glass and glassmaking, and firearms and militia equipment. Visitors can investigate the world of time and high craftsmanship in the Village's renowned exhibition of early New England clocks. Changing exhibitions in the Visitor Center Galleries seek out compelling themes to explore, using the museum's holdings to interpret such topics as the economic and technical transformation of furniture making, the stunning emergence of portrait painting in the countryside, or the remarkably complex ways in which the rural New England of the 1830s was linked to Europe, Latin America, Asia, and the Pacific.

Each exhibit and program at the museum is meticulously grounded in historical research. Curators, historians, and archaeologists work with an enormous variety of sources to trace the lineaments of the everyday American past: the evidence of buildings and archaeological sites; material objects of almost every description; documents ranging from account books, diaries, and letters, to newspapers, census and tax records; and even the "experimental" evidence about crafts processes accumulated by working historical artisans.

New England's people built well, labored hard, and cherished their traditions while looking to the future and the past in nearly equal measure. They surely could not have anticipated the shape of modern society, but they expected change. Their legacy—of lives grounded in work, family, and community, of buildings and objects variously beautiful, functional, and curious, of rock-solid tradition blended with innovative energy—is before us today. It lives still at Old Sturbridge Village.

Jack Larkin
Director, Research, Collections, and Library, Old Sturbridge Village

CHAPTER ONE

Roots of Rural New England

BY 1830 THERE WERE WELL OVER A thousand towns in the New England states of Massachusetts, Connecticut, Rhode Island, Maine, New Hampshire, and Vermont. The inland rural communities were the last to be settled and developed, mostly in the eighteenth century. They comprise the majority of all the region's settlements and are those with which Old Sturbridge Village, as a museum of rural New England life, is most concerned. Sturbridge is located in Massachusetts—in the southwest corner of Worcester County, which stretches in a wide belt across the center of the state. The re-created historical landscape of Old Sturbridge Village portrays the defining features of the New England town and documents how the traditions and changes experienced by the people of rural Worcester County were shared in common with most New Englanders.

The New England landscape of the 1830s had been shaped by the continuous development of agricultural communities since the early seventeenth century. By the time the twenty-year migration of English Puritans subsided after 1642, as many as twenty thousand immigrants—a huge number for the times—had settled there. They laid out permanent fields and built houses, fell into familiar routines of exchange and commerce, and found ready markets for exporting furs, dried fish, and lumber. As these immigrants

Opposite: By the 1830s travelers saw rural New England as a landscape of scattered farms and white-painted villages (Anonymous oil painting, c. 1840)

Above: Baskets like this one, made through much of the nineteenth century for trade with Yankee neighbors, attest to the enduring presence of Native Americans in rural New England

multiplied and extended their claims, the Algonkian-speaking American Indians who had lived in the region for centuries were gradually overwhelmed. Although friendly relations between Native Americans and the Puritans were common enough, tribes that rose in resistance suffered disastrous defeats. Whether through legitimate barter, chicanery, or outright force (most notably in the horrifying bloodshed of "King Philip's War" in 1675–76), the native peoples of New England were ultimately dispossessed and greatly dispersed.

To a large extent New England was not settled by individual adventurers, but by families. For the most part, they were artisans, tradesmen, and farmers, together with their wives, children, dependent relatives, and household servants. Often, whole "dissenting" congregations migrated together under the leadership of a magistrate or minister. They brought a powerful sense of purpose and a deliberate idealism to the shaping of their new society in America.

Their settlements spread out from Plymouth and Massachussetts Bay to what would become Rhode Island, Connecticut, New Hampshire, and Maine. Settlers peopled the coastal plains and river valleys long before they started to fill the hilly, thickly wooded country of central Massachusetts and northeastern Connecticut. Fishing, shipbuilding, and maritime commerce flourished along the coast, but the work that occupied most of New England's people was farming.

The early immigrants brought livestock, tools, crops, and traditions with them to the New World, and their first settlements were simply outposts of rural English society. From the Old World came cattle, sheep, and hogs, and English grains and grasses that were grown alongside American Indian crops—corn, beans, pumpkins, and squash. New England's frigid winters, unpredictable frosts, and hot summers forced anxious adjustments to traditional farming practices. As the great inland forests gradually yielded

A country road leads away from the Freeman Farm. In the 1830s such roads connected farmsteads, neighborhoods, and villages

to land cleared for cultivation, a distinctive pattern of rural settlement, only partly echoing the ways of England, slowly unfolded.

From the earliest days, New England's provincial authorities had attempted to encourage the formation of communities by parceling out large tracts of land to groups of settlers committed to establishing themselves as a religious congregation and as a "town." The first New England communities were closely settled villages, each with a meetinghouse—as the Puritans called their church buildings—and each with a broad belt of farmland surrounding the central settlement. Large outlying tracts of meadows and woodlots were reserved for common use or held for future development. This layout was derived largely from villages in southern England, and it was viewed as a useful way to encourage social order and organize the defense of vulnerable communities. But these arrangements were altered dramatically by the abundance and irresistible enticement of the land.

Over time, farm families preferred to settle on scattered parcels of land with good soil, water, and drainage. They abandoned their village lots around the green or never took them up at all, pressing for a division of the common lands into individual farmsteads. A 1635 law of the Massachusetts General Court requiring town residents to settle within a half mile of the meetinghouse had been so widely flouted that it was repealed only five years later. Eventually, most of the large tracts held in common were sold off. Over the next two centuries, New Englanders organized their settlements in a plan that became traditional, with meetinghouse and common near the center and home-steads spreading out across the landscape in an expanding patchwork of cleared land. An eighteenth-century town center with only a meetinghouse, an inn, a school, and a dwelling or two was often the heart of a substantial community of farms, small mills, and scattered shops.

A network of primitive roads gradually extended over southern New England during the eighteenth century, bringing scattered farming families to the meetinghouse and opening the channels of commerce. In virtually every rural community, most house-holds became involved in trade with the wider world. Surplus cheese, butter, livestock, and grain trickled out of the countryside to Boston and other market towns. In return, "assortments for the country trade" met the modest demands of rural households: spices, rum, sugar and tea, tobacco, window glass, hardware, teapots, cutlery, buttons, and even a few trappings of fashion.

Most country roads ran to the town center like spokes to the hub of a wheel. They carried countryfolk from outlying farms on their traditional weekly visit to "town," to attend meeting, stop at the tavern, or trade with the small shops and country stores that had begun to locate near the common later in the eighteenth century. While farm-steads were not gathered into villages, they were rarely located more than half a mile from their nearest neighbors, usually scattered along the road or gathered in twos or threes at a crossroads. Although substantial tracts of wooded land were evident well into the nineteenth century, most farmers had cleared enough of their fields and pasture so that neighboring houses were visible. Almost all families farmed, but the small shops of part-time artisans—potters, wheelwrights, tanners, blacksmiths, and woodworkers—were found in every town, along with small water-powered gristmills and sawmills.

The people of New England remained, even into the nineteenth century, the most homo-geneous of all Americans. In 1790, some 80 percent were of English descent, and most were descended from the original Puritan settlers. Around 15 percent were of Welsh, Scottish, or early Protestant Irish stock. Until about 1820, when the Catholic Irish immi-grants began coming in larger numbers, the only visibly defined minorities in the area were African-Americans and Native Americans, who together comprised at least 2 per-cent of the total population. New England's "free colored" African-Americans were the descendants of the region's slaves, the great majority of whom were freed between 1780 and 1810. Occasionally, free blacks farmed their own land or worked at skilled trades, but mostly they survived as laborers and tenant farmers. Some Native Americans con-founded expectations, getting by in the larger communities. But more often they lived in enclaves on scattered ancestral "reserves" or shared the life of small neighbor-hoods with other "people of color." Although antislavery sentiment was stronger in New England than in any other part of the country, and both groups had lived in rural communities for generations, they continued to face barriers of racial prejudice and discrimination.

Rural New Englanders did share, with few exceptions, a daily life that by today's standards was characterized by discomfort, austerity, and long hours of hard work. Drafty homes were heated by inefficient fireplaces, and meals were cooked labo-

riously over open fires. Although food was quite plentiful, it was often monotonous—salt pork, dried beans, brown bread and milk, and hard cider. Water for drinking, cooking, or washing was drawn by bucket from a spring or a well. Bathing was virtually unknown, and indoor plumbing consisted of a chamber pot under the bed. Candles and the flickering hearth were the only sources of artificial light.

Country life was intensely local. The scattered farms and shops of the countryside were roughly divided into neighborhood settlements, areas of a few square miles marked by a schoolhouse, a country crossroads, and sometimes a mill or two. They usually took their names—for example, "Fiske Hill," "Four Corners," or "Wyman's Mills"—from features of local geography or genealogy. These neighborhoods remained predominantly agricultural, and they encompassed the immediate social and economic worlds of most New Englanders, even as their role in commerce and market production expanded during the early nineteenth century. They were the actual localities that made up a town's intricate social reality, and they were bound together by social rituals such as visiting, quiltings, huskings, and dances, as well as by the complex ties of kinship. Places often retained their identification with one or two original families for generations.

Neighborhoods were sometimes defined by religious affiliation. The Congregational Church, as the descendants of Puritans came to call the assemblies of their tradition, remained throughout the Colonial years the dominant, government-supported denomination throughout most of New England. Dissenters were usually more comfortable living near one another and somewhat removed from the Congregational meetinghouse at the town center. In the eighteenth century the Friends, or Quakers, often settled in secluded locations, built their own meetinghouses, and maintained separate schools and graveyards. The Baptists of Sturbridge originally followed this pattern in living

together on the slope of Fiske Hill well away from the town common, raising their meet-inghouse close to a bend in the Quinebaug River. Even later-emerging dissenting groups such as Methodists and Universalists frequently built their chapels and meetinghouses in outlying districts.

The cohesion of neighborhoods was further strengthened by New England's system of country schooling. Depending on their size, towns were divided into six to fif-teen rural school districts. Drawn to keep the children's journeys as short as possible, districts usually covered an area of about two to four square miles. Each district reflected and defined a particular neighborhood's patterns of kinship, visiting, and trading. From locating, building, and repairing a one-room schoolhouse to the hiring and boarding of teachers, local interest in the management of district schools ran very high. Schoolhouses were usually the only public buildings outside the town centers, so it was not unusual for them to serve as meeting places for singing schools, religious assemblies, and other communal activities.

New England's traditional rural economy was concentrated in settlements and neigh-borhoods. Families sought a "competency," or comfortable subsistence, that they might pass on to their children, but they very rarely sought a household "self-sufficiency." Instead, they participated with their nearby kin and neighbors in intricate and enduring networks of exchange for needed goods or labor and the use of tools and livestock.

Even after longer-distance marketing of farm goods came to characterize the rural economy, extensive webs of local trading continued to provide a significant degree of self-sufficiency at the neighborhood level. Strongly enmeshed in exchange networks every-where were the country artisans, who created most of the material goods and specialized services that were available in rural areas. Millers and sawyers, blacksmiths and house-wrights, shoemakers and potters usually combined their valuable trades with farming on some scale and transmitted their versions of the old English skills to their sons or nephews.

The most commonly surviving records of the ordinary people of rural New England are account books—records kept by most farmers and craftsmen to keep track of a web of exchanges with relatives, neighbors, and some customers farther away. Families exchanged skilled services, farm and household labor, many kinds of produce, and the use of their tools, vehicles, animals, and land. The accounts are single-entry ledgers, usually assigning debits and credits on a pair of opposing pages to record transactions with another household or tradesman.

This widespread vernacular bookkeeping was far more prevalent in New England than anywhere else in rural America, and it became close to universal among ordinary farmers and craftsmen during the late eighteenth and early nineteenth centuries. Cash payments were relatively rare, but transactions were reckoned according to prices widely known and accepted—prices that distantly reflected those of urban markets. So traditional was the habit of reckoning that accounts were often recorded in "colonial" shillings and pence long after dollars and cents had become the standard currency. Each "settling" between neighbors, sometimes occurring on New Year's Day, was both a ritual affirmation of the ongoing reciprocity of the relationship and a hard-eyed reckoning of the current balance. These account books say little about profit and loss in a modern sense, but they tell us a great deal about enduring social and economic connections.

Life at the end of the eighteenth century was considerably more comfortable than it had been earlier in the seventeenth. Yet the basic patterns of life deeply rooted in agriculture and craftsmanship and driven by the cycle of the seasons remained. For the most part, the daily tasks of every farming household were performed by hand: mowing hay, picking stones, husking corn, felling trees, digging beets, churning butter, pressing cheese, hilling potatoes, spinning wool. By and large, women laid claim to hearth, home, and garden, while men attended to barnyards, fields, and doings in the greater world.

Up through the end of the eighteenth century, the traditional tools, methods of work, and sources of power changed very little. Waterpower drove small neighborhood mills for grinding grain, sawing lumber, or fulling handwoven cloth. Farmers worked with heavy implements of local manufacture; plows and shovels were massive wooden contrivances clad with iron. Oxen were used for the heaviest tasks: dragging loads of timber and stones, pulling plows and harrows, and hauling in the harvest.

In the half century following George Washington's inauguration in 1789, the rural New England landscape changed dramatically. As the countryside filled with farmsteads, good land became scarcer. In older settlements, most young people wanting to stay in farming had to move north or west. Farmers gradually cleared their previously unimproved lands by opening up ever steeper slopes for pasture and hay. Steadily, panoramic views of a new landscape were revealed on every side. Stone walls and fence lines meandered out to edge the rolling fields or to lace between the woodlots and the orchards. Narrow ribbons of road snaked from farm to farm, converging finally near a town common where the meetinghouse spire rose up tall and white.

The once sparsely settled town centers now began to bustle with artisans, pro-

Lowell, Massachusetts, and hundreds of smaller manufacturing communities drew thousands of young women and whole families from their farms to the new world of the factory

The Freeman Farm at dusk. Illumination was far dimmer in early America and nights much darker

fessionals, and shopkeepers. The first mechanized cotton-spinning factory was set up in a converted mill in Pawtucket, Rhode Island, in 1793. Soon, small manufacturing villages were sprouting up along streams and rivers, at almost any site where waterpower could be harnessed; they became magnets for country people, mostly women and children from poorer families, who were recruited to tend the new machines. Some of these communities became true cities. By 1833, the textile mills of Lowell, Massachusetts, alone employed some six thousand workers. Nearly all farming households discovered a chance for greater prosperity in the steadily expanding markets for produce that the growing commercial and manufacturing villages created.

The Industrial Revolution came to America in the form of adapted British technology and creative methods of organizing handwork. Until about 1820, textile factories harnessed waterpower only to spin cotton, while the weaving work was still being "put out" to nearby households. By the 1830s, after power looms for weaving cotton and wool were available, the mechanization of textile production was virtually complete. Yankee farm girls were recruited to work in the larger factories, while entire families provided the labor for smaller mills.

By then, New England shops and factories were churning out everything from brass buttons and tacks to clock parts and gun barrels. Artisans who traditionally had supplied their local neighborhoods with made-to-order products were soon being undersold by the new producers of standardized goods. The more enterprising among them opened shops in the villages or took on a worker or two in the countryside. They made

furniture, printed books, built wagons, and forged scythe blades, axes, clock parts, or plough beams. Mass production and the division of labor came to these trades well before mechanization. Opportunities for "industrial" work in the countryside multiplied dramatically.

Production expanded to meet the growing demand for goods throughout the nation—and even abroad. In New England's "sale shoe" industry, young men worked at "bottoming" shoes in thousands of tiny shops scattered throughout the region, while women sewed the uppers at home. Sturdy men's shoes were the most common product in the central part of the region, while eastern Massachusetts specialized in making women's footwear. This mass-production shoemaking, requiring only a few months of training, was organized by enterprising merchant/manufacturers, who supplied their workers with all materials and paid for the finished goods in cash.

Many wives and daughters—actually far outnumbering the women who had gone off to the mills—discovered a new source of income in the variety of "outwork" available in central New England. Besides "fitting" shoe uppers, they were braiding straw, making palm-leaf hats, and occasionally rushing and caning chairs. Others were

Part of the economic revolution that transformed the countryside—a rural furniture manufacturer's house, shop, and salesroom (Anonymous oil painting, c.1833)

employed painting tinware and clock dials. By the 1830s, few families seemed to be beyond the newly extended reach of cash and commerce.

Many other changes in traditional ways followed in the wake of the great transformation in methods and markets. An economy based on neighborhood exchange gradually began to break down with the increase of cash in circulation. Progressive agricultural writers even argued that exchanges of labor, "frolics," and huskings—traditional rituals of cooperative work in farming communities—were inefficient and wasteful, and many farmers began to agree. Eventually, the account book world, with its mingling of trading and visiting, disappeared. Many kinds of production once carried on in rural households withered away as the new factories flourished. First spinning wheels and then looms became rare in southern New England homes, and bread grains and flax gradually vanished from the fields. Rural blacksmiths concentrated on repairs as the demand for handmade tools and implements declined. In some trades, larger shops and the division of labor eroded the apprentice-journeyman system. Traditional redware potters and cabinetmakers, unable to compete with the makers of cheaper, mass-produced chairs or tinware, began to diminish in number.

The revolution in manufacturing was unleashed by significant improvements in transportation. New England towns and counties had long been responsible for maintaining roadways, but in the 1790s there was a great rush to charter private companies to build and maintain toll roads along important routes of travel. By 1800, two-thirds of the nation's seventy-two "turnpikes" were in New England. Toll road fervor ended around 1820, but the "passion for improving roads" did not. The plodding two-wheeled oxcarts of 1800 gave way to the heavily loaded four-wheeled horse-drawn wagons of the 1830s. Out into the countryside went ever larger quantities of manufactured goods, both domestic and imported—spirits, sugar, fish, and even flour. Back into the cities came butter, cheese, hay, and rural manufactures. Overland freight costs remained high by the later standards set by the railroads—about $10 per ton for the fifty miles from Worcester to

Boston—but speed and convenience, for freight and passengers alike, improved dramatically. In 1790 the trip to New York from Boston took at least four days, six if the weather was bad. By 1833, commercial stagecoaches, traveling even at night, covered the distance in less than thirty-four hours.

The opening of the Erie Canal system in 1825 had a galvanizing effect on the nation's trade, as western farm produce began flowing east in exchange for the shoes, merchandise, and hardware of New England. Freight shipments between the Great Lakes and New York suddenly required only six days instead of twenty, and the cost for shipping grain dropped from $100 to $8 a ton. The wheat and flour coming through Buffalo soon surpassed amounts being shipped by sea through New Orleans. By 1840, the traditional bread grains of New England—even for many farm families—had been replaced by cheaper, high-quality wheat flour from the fertile soils of western New York and Ohio.

In 1830, the most startling marvel of the whole "breathless" age came puffing along thirteen miles of track outside Baltimore. The new "rail way" was incredibly fast, up to twenty miles per hour! Although railroads were more expensive to operate than canals, they were cheaper to build and did not freeze over in the winter. Short runs of iron track radiated out from cities practically overnight, and within ten years track mileage across the country had overtaken the canals. The Boston and Worcester Railway opened in 1835 in the face of vigorous opposition from owners of the stage lines, who could see that their popular day-and-a-half run to New York was about to seem dreadfully slow.

In Colonial times, New England, like other British settlements in North America, had abounded in children. Until late in the eighteenth century, rural families averaged eight or so apiece, creating an explosive growth of population that mirrored that of the developing world today. But even this long-enduring pattern began to change as part of the countryside's economic and social transformation. Starting in the decades after the Revolution, New England family size grew gradually smaller. As the farming

economy reached saturation, land on which to settle succeeding generations of children grew scarce and costly.

Young couples grew more concerned about establishing their children in the emerging new world of commerce and industrial enterprise. They chose to marry later and limit their fertility, as New England led the nation into "modern" ideas about family size. By 1840, rural families averaged around five-and-a-half children each—still large by today's standards but strikingly smaller than those of earlier generations.

For generations, before the bustle of commerce swept through the villages, a stark and rustic subsistence had prevailed in the countryside. Farmers had enjoyed a slowly rising prosperity throughout the Colonial years, but the everyday demands of living and working on the land placed severe limitations on "refinements" in outlying households. The assets of ordinary farmsteads were tied up in land, livestock, and equipment, and scant attention was paid to finish and adornment. Even by 1800, few country dwellings could boast a grassy lawn or dooryard fence. More often than not, the treeless house lots were simply bare and trampled earth or choked with uncut weeds. Privies, located with an offhand practicality, were conspicuous features of the landscape. Families lived in a close and daily involvement with their livestock, and most dooryards were casually littered with trash and old tools. "Bits of wood, timber, boards and chips lying about," were among the vivid memories of one Englishman's visit to New England. New Haven clock-maker Chauncey Jerome remembered the enormous, tangled piles of firewood—"the loads of wood and chips for family use"—that stood heaped near many a door.

Most of the dwellings on these rough properties were small, with large fireplaces and single chimneys. A rare housing inventory, the Direct Tax of 1798, revealed that some two-thirds of the dwellings in Worcester County in Massachusetts were single-story, with one in four being worth less than $100. For the most part, these houses were left unpainted, and the weather-stained, clapboard siding customarily described as "brown." The survey used such words as "indifferent," "small and mean," or "poor and old" to describe many of the houses.

Indoors, ceilings were often low, furnishings usually sparse, and floors and windows unadorned. Carpets were rare and cushioned furniture even rarer, while chairs did not always number enough to seat every member of the household. Fewer than one home in ten had an image of any kind on its walls, although many more might boast a looking glass or two. Large families and relatively small houses meant that rooms were crowded and beds were shared. The work of the household, from preparing food to making cloth, intruded everywhere upon spaces used for sleeping, eating, and socializing. Even the parlor might have a bed in it and be cluttered with milk pans, drying apples, and skeins of woolen yarn.

By the 1830s, however, the signs of growing rural prosperity could be clearly seen. New Englanders were still lighting the darkness with candles, heating with wood, using privies, and hauling water; but the new technologies had generated a growing abundance for ordinary people and heightened their aspirations for improvement and "gentility." Two-story houses became more common, just as the size of the family was growing smaller. Rooms less often served a hodgepodge of uses, and the prospects for

privacy, and even for bathing, were much improved. Piles of firewood were more often neatly stacked and kitchen gardens carefully tended. Lots were edged with fences and dooryards tidied up. Trash was discarded with greater care, yards were weeded, and flowers planted. Local improvement societies encouraged the planting of shade trees around homes, on town commons, and along nearby roads. As house after house throughout the countryside was painted with the newly affordable white lead paint, an orderly domestic landscape emerged as the enduring symbol of New England life.

The prosperity of farmsteads increasingly depended upon a combination of farming with part-time trades and outwork, while the new wealth of the villages was built upon trade and manufacturing. The prosperous people of the villages came to dominate social life, and they invariably played leadership roles in local politics and church affairs. They initiated and supported the broad array of voluntary associations that sprang up in rural communities—charitable societies and missionary associations, tree-planting committees, antislavery and moral improvement societies, Masonic lodges, and lyceums. "Americans . . .," noted Alexis de Tocqueville in 1831, "are forever forming associations," and nowhere was this observation more perfectly realized than in the thriving communities of rural New England.

The new economy also brought a truly astonishing revolution in the varieties of goods and furnishings available to ordinary people. Clothing and shoes became far more abundant, and the new power looms brought the cost of a parlor carpet within the reach of over 20 percent of rural households. Household inventories show substantial increases over time in the ownership of chairs—now mass-produced in water-powered shops— tables, looking glasses, and, to a lesser extent, candlesticks. Farmhouse interiors were

brightened by more candles, and many village households were buying new oil lamps—fueling the growth of New England's whaling industry. After 1820, cookstoves slowly began to replace kitchen hearths, and sofas and other cushioned furniture became the new symbols of gentility and comfort. Images of any kind had once been rare and expensive, but many householders were now commissioning portraits by itinerant painters and decorated their walls with engravings and amateur schoolgirl cuts. Clocks, with wooden works, brought timekeeping into at least half of rural homes. A few families were even able to afford the ultimate extravagance—a pianoforte.

New Englanders shared unevenly in these new comforts and domestic improvements, however. There had always been contrasts between the poorest and most prosperous neighborhoods in rural communities. Sometimes, thanks to the unpredictable distribution of productive lands, well-to-do farmers lived side by side with neighbors barely making a living. In other communities, prosperous clusters of large, two-story homes and substantial New England barns contrasted sharply with straggling settlements of small unpainted houses and ramshackle sheds. These divergences had become more apparent by the 1830s, sometimes suggesting that people were living in different centuries. The "old manners" attached themselves to rural poverty and isolation, while the new prosperity seemed to betoken "city ways."

The new furnishings and standards of gentility were adopted rapidly by commercial and professional families in villages and more gradually and unevenly by the countryfolk. By the 1830s, many rustic pockets of the old austerity still remained, but the steady march toward refinement was widespread and impressive. Interestingly, some of the loudest champions of rural improvement—editors, ministers, gentleman farmers—began to wonder if things hadn't gone too far. By 1832, articles in the *New England Farmer* were maintaining that farmers and rural mechanics were building their houses "too large for comfort, convenience or beauty" and paying too much attention to comfort and luxury. Already, there was some uneasiness about the burgeoning affluence wrought by commerce and the new machines, and some nostalgia for the habits and sufficiencies of country ways that were starting to vanish.

The bustling 1830s did, in fact, set in motion the gradual disappearance of the old handmade world in New England, where people worked to the cycle of the seasons and passed their lives in the close, familiar spheres of neighborhoods and country towns. The economic and social transformation of the early nineteenth century reshaped the entire fabric of life through countless adjustments and small changes, repeated in thousands of families and neighborhoods throughout every community. How the great changes of the age—and sometimes its turmoil—penetrated the modest and usually undramatic lives of rural New Englanders was evident everywhere—in letters and diaries, in dooryards and parlors, in workshops and stores, all along the dusty roads, and in the pounding mills. Today, through the active and deeply interwoven displays of historic buildings, objects, and demonstrations at Old Sturbridge Village, we can look back just once more at the now vanished landscapes and changing times of a rural community in the 1830s.

Decorative family records set down the minute details of birth, marriage, and death for proud display in thousands of New England households

CHAPTER TWO

Farms

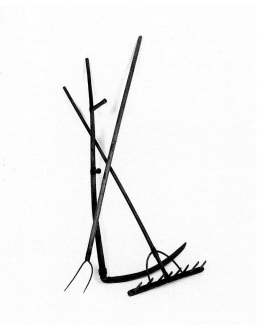

AGRICULTURE BOUND TOGETHER THE PASS-
ing generations of New Englanders and harmonized their
increasing diversity. Together, the rich and the poor—
and even most city dwellers—had at least spent their
childhoods in the countryside. Not only country artisans,
but even many ministers, doctors, lawyers, and storekeepers and their wives had grown up on the farm. By the
opening of the nineteenth century, some 250 farms, connected by the web of roads radiating from the center village, shaped the patchwork landscape of a typical town.
Farming was still the largest sector in the economy by far
in the 1830s, even though commerce and industry had
expanded dramatically. Farmers continued to follow the
traditional patterns of English agriculture as they had
been adapted by their ancestors to New England conditions. From their European inheritance came wheat, rye, oats, and barley, plus English grasses for hay, along with cattle,
sheep, pigs, horses, and poultry. Adopted native crops of beans, squash, and pumpkins
had developed into traditional mainstays as well, and one in particular—"Indian" corn—
became the single most important grain crop of the New England farm.

Farming knowledge—of crops and livestock, of shifting weather patterns and
the onset of the seasons, of tasks and tools, and even superstitions—was passed on from
one generation to the next. Centuries-old routines of agricultural work endured with little change into the early years of the nineteenth century. Plowing, planting, cultivating,
and harvesting dominated farming life from early spring to late in the fall. Winter
allowed some time for leisure and social visiting, but many chores—cutting timber, tending livestock, and making repairs—still beckoned. Oxen were used to pull plows and

*Opposite: Preoccupied with work, New
England farmers rarely commented on
the beauty of their landscape. But a view
like this might have made them pause for
a moment*

*Above: The tools of husbandry: dung
fork for spreading manure, scythe with
curved snath for cutting hay, and rake for
spreading and gathering hay*

harrows, skid logs, and haul heavy loads, yet a great measure of daily farmwork could only be accomplished through massive human effort. With virtually no machinery, using only a traditional array of hand tools, New England farmers mowed hay, reaped and thrashed grain, picked stones and hoed corn, split rails and hauled potatoes, spread manure and husked corn. Most farming households subsisted on a day-to-day basis largely outside the cash economy, producing a broad range of diversified crops and products and exchanging goods and labor with neighboring farmers and tradesmen.

During the second and third decades of the new century, however, as transportation continually improved, national markets emerged, and new industries proliferated, the pace of change quickened even for tradition-bound farmers. They steadily increased their production for the market and began to adopt new tools and techniques as well. Wooden tools that customarily had only been edged with iron were now being turned out with greater portions of cast iron, combining redesigned shapes and stronger handles. "Common" farmers took up the new tools only very cautiously, but many of the "great" farmers and their hired hands were working with an entire collection of new implements by the 1830s.

By 1839, the *Farmer's Almanack* could declare that since the beginning of the century there was "scarcely a tool that has not been altered for the better in some way or other." Hand-cranked fanning mills appeared, replacing the age-old practice of winnowing by throwing grain up in the open air to separate the seeds from the chaff. Many dairy operations adopted mechanical butter churns and cheese presses. "Progressive" agricultural practices were widely advocated in periodical publications and pamphlets and promoted at agricultural society meetings. Farmers responded by giving up their old wasteful ways of managing the soil, which customarily left many worn-out fields fallow for a decade. They adopted crop rotation and the use of root crops, lime, and heavy manuring to improve fertility.

Expanding cities, manufacturing hamlets, and center villages began to provide "home markets in every valley" for New England farmers. Most farmers, especially those with large, prosperous operations like the one depicted at Old Sturbridge Village for Salem Towne, Jr., began to adjust their production to the growing trade. They concentrated more of their resources on producing for sale—selling hay, beef, pork, butter, and cheese through local markets, storekeepers, and marketmen; sending livestock to Boston or New York; and sometimes even supplying wool to nearby textile mills. Even farmers of more moderate means, like Pliny Freeman, whose farm is portrayed at the museum, were increasing their flocks and expanding their dairies. Many New England farmers had complemented their agricultural work with other part-time endeavors, such as carpentry, coopering, pottery, or blacksmithing. Some responded to changing opportunities by expanding these activities or finding new ones, such as "sale" shoemaking. Although farmers prospered less visibly than many residents of the flourishing center villages, they nonetheless enjoyed the benefits of the new commercial economy.

The Freeman Farm

Overleaf: The Freeman Farm in early summer

Of the historical persons associated with the buildings at Old Sturbridge Village, more is known about Pliny Freeman and his family than most others. He was a farmer of the "middling class or sort," and we have every reason to assume that he was a strong traditionalist. Such men farmed much as their fathers had before them. Having neither the inclination nor the money to experiment with untried and risky new ideas, they worked

to secure a comfortable sufficiency—or "competence"—for their families and to help their children get established in life. Throughout his life, Freeman farmed his modest acreage with an eye to the marketplace. He increased production of wool and cheese for market, bought more land, and took on such other work as opportunity, and his versatile skills, allowed. He sometimes worked as a housewright, owned part-interest in a sawmill for several years, bottomed shoes, and made and sold ox yokes. Many thousands of farmers across New England remained on New England soil by following similar strategies. Others made even more momentous choices, as agricultural opportunity beckoned from farther away. Pliny's brother, Samuel, had farmed for decades on their father's old place. But he found it "a hard farm from which to obtain a livelihood," as his son remembered, and in 1825 he pulled up stakes and moved to Ohio.

The Freeman Farm's re-created landscape is parceled into woodlot, pasture, hay or "mowing," and tillage. On a long-established farm of middling size, seventy to one hundred acres, a third of the property or so should be woodland, used to supply firewood, fencing, and building lumber. New England farmers had little difficulty in supplying their own needs for wood, but the cost of lumber and firewood in the growing villages and cities rose as farmers cleared their forested holdings, opening up more and more land. Another third of the farm, mostly marginal fields and rocky hillsides, might be in pasture, where livestock grazed for the summer.

Of the remaining land, a small parcel of about two or three acres—sometimes a bit more—would be taken up by the house and barn, outbuildings and barnyards, orchard and kitchen garden. About twenty-five acres would be marked off for growing hay, in many ways New England's most important crop. The hayfields were sown with "English" grasses—timothy, redtop, and orchard grass—plus clover and trefoil, crops that were more nutritious for livestock than the native grasses that grew in the pastures. Six to twelve acres of good tillage were needed for growing field crops. Wheat, vul-

nerable to insects and fungus, did not grow well in most of southern New England. But Indian corn, rye, oats, potatoes, and small amounts of barley and buckwheat flourished. With virtually no machinery and only such labor as could be found in the family or exchanged with neighbors, the middling farm of the early nineteenth century stayed small.

The first chores of spring at the Freeman Farm are repairing winter-weakened fences and hauling dung into still-frozen fields. As soon as the ground is dry enough, the farmers can be seen, day after day, following behind a heavy ox-drawn plow to prepare fields for planting. Hay crops and oats are usually sown first, followed by potatoes and then corn. Following the traditional practice, farmers plow and cross-plow the Freeman fields, then smooth out the tumbled heaps and clods by dragging heavy brushwood harrows across the soil. For corn and potatoes, furrows and cross-furrows are then plowed at three- or four-foot intervals across the fields, and seeds are planted in hills left by the intersecting rows. Once the plants come up, a long summer's work of cultivation begins as plow and hoe are used to kill weeds and draw up "hills" of earth around the base of the plants. "This work can hardly be, and seldom is finished," commented New England's pioneering agricultural writer, Samuel Deane, "before the grass on the high lands calls for mowing."

Haying season arrives in late June and continues through early August. In the

Opposite: Two teams of oxen are hitched together for heavy plowing

Above: Bringing in the hay, "the most rushed and anxious task of summer," on the Freeman Farm

Opposite above: Spring plowing in the Fitch House garden

Opposite below: Harvesting rye in the field beyond the Fenno Barn

Right: Warming up by the fire after winter chores

Following pages: The Freeman Farm's cattle yard, the Cooper Shop, and the farm's tillage fields beyond

1830s, it was a time of such urgency that it occupied every available hand in the neighborhood—farmer, tradesman, merchant, or clerk—in several weeks of exhausting labor. Young men, in particular, found it a time to demonstrate their strength and skill. To be named best mower in the neighborhood might count as much to some as the high wages—one dollar per day and occasionally more—that this great labor could command. Mowing starts in the early cool of the morning, as the haying crews move out across the fields in an urgent battle "against the heat and the rain and the legions of timothy and clover." With the continuous, rhythmic swinging of their long-handled scythes, several mowers in a row lay down swath after swath of long, dewy grass behind their glittering blades. They mow as steadily and as fast as they can, stopping only briefly to sharpen their blades with whetstones and take a refreshing swig. Early-nineteenth-century mowers usually preferred rum or hard cider, but temperance-minded employers were beginning to offer nonalcoholic "switchel" or even cold water as a substitute.

Before the heat of the day has passed, mowers must spread, turn, and rake the hay into windrows and then roll it into cocks, or small piles, to minimize damage from rain or dew. After that, they are wise to begin hauling in whatever hay is dry from the previous day's cutting, filling the mows in the barn or stacking it in the yard. Because hay was essential for keeping livestock over the winter, it was more important to the farm's survival than any other crop. Once mowing had begun, any mismanagement or delay could have costly consequences: good farmers made ready well in advance an extra supply of scythes and blades, pitchforks, and rake handles. To avoid the loss of a crucial crop to impending rain, farm women might sometimes be called into the fields to help rake and cock the hay. With time taken out for rainy days and—almost always—for Sabbaths, the exhausting work and hurry of haying time in New England made it the season that "tries the religion of farmers," according to the Reverend Timothy Richardson.

Two or three weeks into July, when most of the upland hay had been secured, New England farmers would typically turn their attention to crops of small grains: rye and oats, sometimes wheat or barley. Rye was always sown in the winter and was normally the first to be harvested. At the Freeman Farm, rye is cut with short-handled "reaping hooks" that allow the farmers to take hold of the stalks in small bundles and cut them carefully without shattering the well-ripened heads. The rye is then lifted up, bound into sheaves, and stood up in shocks to dry. Oats were sometimes harvested in the same way, but the Freeman farmers use another equally common method—cutting the grain with a scythe before it is fully ripe and drying it loose like hay. This preserves more straw and loses less grain while getting it into the barn.

After the grain has been harvested, farmers return to their mowing and cultivating. In August and September they finish up the mowing, plow their rye fields for winter planting, and start to dig potatoes. As the fall season deepens, ripened ears of corn are finally picked and carted in from the fields in load after load. The cornstalks, either cut down or left standing, are fed to livestock. Apples are picked and hauled away for pressing at the Cider Mill, and pumpkins are collected from the cornfields. Grain is threshed on the barn floor with wooden flails and winnowed in the open entryway with a fan or basket.

Later in the fall and into the winter, the work of husking and shelling corn remains. Because husking was a tedious chore for each family on its own, New Englanders had a long tradition of husking "frolics" that brought neighbors together for festive gatherings of cooperative work. More "progressive" farmers of the 1830s were abandoning them, saying that they were occasions for drinking, clowning, and inefficiency. But the old ways lingered among many "common" farmers. The slow winter months of the early nineteenth century were times for leisure and socializing, but always there were—and are—chores and projects to be finished. As temperatures plunge and snow arrives on howling winds, farmers skid logs from the woodlots, split firewood, make fencing stock, repair their tools, and slaughter livestock. They cut spiles, make troughs, and sled wood to the "sugar camp" in preparation for maple sugaring in March.

The Freeman Farm still follows these seasonal rhythms and evokes the nearly lost world of an early farmstead. Fresh meadow breezes mingle with the sharp, musty smells of a working barnyard. Bits of straw and hay blow through the open driveway of the barn, and buckets of sweet, warm milk stand ready for hauling to the dairy. Field crops and garden vegetables are fresh, but also old—to every extent possible, they are the traditional varieties originally grown in the New England countryside.

Caring for livestock is year-round work. Feeding the animals and cleaning their stalls and sheds, attending to their breeding and births, shearing the sheep, milking the cows, and training young oxen to the yoke were common doings of everyday life in the nineteenth century. Most of the livestock raised on New England farms were "native" descendants of animals brought over from England during the initial decades of settlement. They were "common" cattle, sheep, swine, and poultry, not of any particular breed. "Dunghill" fowl were speckled and nondescript. Common sheep were hardy creatures with small fleeces. Cattle were the most often described, with their size, color, and markings sometimes noted in farm inventories and occasionally illustrated in paintings.

Livestock at the Freeman Farm today are themselves living historical documents, carefully bred to resemble their early-nineteenth-century predecessors in size, shape, and coloring.

In many ways, the story of the Freeman Farm in the 1830s was typical of the New England experience. As successive, ever-larger generations of New Englanders appeared, and the landscape filled with farms, it had become harder to pass on an enduring connection to the land. Pliny, unlike his father or grandfather before him, did not have enough land to establish his children on their own farms. His sons and sons-in-law often labored for other farmers. One drove a stage route, one took up the housewright's craft, and another went to work making shoes. Ultimately, only one son stayed on in the Sturbridge area. Family letters tell of the death of daughter Beulah by lightning in 1835. All the other children eventually headed west to the promising lands of Ohio and Illinois.

Above left: The driveway or "pass-through" of the Freeman Barn. Milking stalls are to the left, and the hay mows above are full

Above right: Husking corn, a tedious task sometimes enlivened by husking frolics. By the 1830s, farmers were advised to go it alone

The Salem Towne Farm

At the 1823 fair of the Worcester County Agricultural Society, Salem Towne, Jr., received a prize for his outstanding Merino ewes. This breed, introduced from Spain during the first decade of the nineteenth century in response to demand from the emerging woolen textile industry, produced a finer grade of wool than could be obtained from native sheep. The flock of Merinos displayed today at the Towne Farm, with their finely textured yet thick and abundant fleeces, bears a strong resemblance to those Towne kept in Charlton, Massachusetts, in the 1820s and 1830s. The cattle in the walled yard near

Opposite: A progressive farmer's improved cattle—Devon-Shorthorn cows on the Salem Towne Farm

the barn are equally representative of Towne's progressive ideas: many of them have imported Durham, or Shorthorn, blood added to the Devon stock that resembles early New England's "native" cattle. In the early nineteenth century, it was well known that the versatile Shorthorn produced good milk cows as well as steers that fattened quickly to marketable weights. Towne was well aware of the advantages of improved breeds. His own herds were extensive, and he was a respected judge of cattle at county and state shows. He maintained a herd that usually numbered over twenty head for an operation that required the milking of fifteen cows or so in peak season.

Unlike Pliny Freeman, enterprising farmers such as Towne traded goods and services in a web of exchange that extended into adjoining towns, and they regularly sent their livestock, cheese, and other products to markets in cities like Boston and Worcester. Such men were at the leading edge of change in New England agriculture, striving to make farming a rational and up-to-date enterprise like commerce, manufacturing, and the professions. To sustain expanded production, they hauled large quantities of manure, used lime to "sweeten" the acid soil, practiced deeper plowing and an elaborate rotation of crops, and perhaps even experimented with the mangel-wurzel root for livestock feed. Progressive farmers kept records of crop yields and meat weights, assessed their expenses against shifting market returns, and worked continually to improve the quality and useful management of their fields and crops, livestock, and fruits. They founded and joined the county, and sometimes local, agricultural societies that advocated and publicized progressive techniques, and they subscribed to the agricultural journals just appearing in the

1820s. They wrote articles, letters to the editor, and corresponded widely, sharing improved crop and fruit varieties, more productive ways to cultivate and enrich the soil, and better techniques of management.

Towne's farm was commensurately larger than Freeman's in the 1830s. Even if Towne had not been busy with public offices and distant business interests, managing his three hundred acres of land and tending his cattle and other livestock would have required help. Like other large-scale farmers, he would have been planting some thirty acres in corn, oats, rye, and root crops and mowing nearly seventy acres of hay. In the summer haying season, Towne would have needed to augment his year-round help with local laborers and even transients hired to work by the day or job. The Towne Farm at the Village is less complete than the Freeman Farm; aside from an orchard, it does not include land under cultivation. It does provide a look at a progressive farmer's operation, with its improved livestock, carefully laid out fencing, and evidence of the newest technologies.

Redesigned tools provide one measure of the changes progressive farmers wrought. They were abandoning the implements of traditional agriculture as heavy, clumsy, and inefficient. Old wooden shovels "shod" with iron edges were replaced by new, lightweight versions with sturdy iron blades and reinforced handles. By 1836, the three Massachusetts factories of Oliver Ames were turning out almost five hundred shovels a day. The unwieldy manure forks made by local blacksmiths could hardly compare with the new Goodyear forks, which were "in no way liable to foul or clog," according to advertisements in the *New England Seed Store Catalog.* Lighter, fine-pronged rakes replaced old handmade designs with thick iron teeth set in wooden crossbars, and factory-made hoes with gooseneck shanks and hardened blades were turned out by the dozens and sold in country stores.

Opposite:

Top left: A hand-cranked fanning mill, an early-nineteenth-century device that mechanized the ancient process of winnowing grain

Top right: The most significant improvement in agricultural New England's farming tools before 1840 was the cast-iron plow, made in specialized shops across the countryside

Bottom left: Another new implement of the 1830s—a commercially made cultivator with cast-iron teeth for cultivating corn and other row crops

Bottom right: Fodder (straw) chopper and corn sheller. Such devices mechanized what had previously been tedious hand operations

Merino ewes and lambs, an improved breed of the 1830s, at the Salem Towne Farm

Scythes with curved "snaths," or handles, which enabled mowers to work in a less tiresome posture, were first made for sale by Silas Lamson in Sterling, Massachusetts. The grain cradle, first used in the mid-Atlantic, was a scythe with a framework of long wooden fingers attached to catch the grain as it was cut. Its use required greater strength and skill than the sickle, but it doubled a reaper's coverage from half an acre to a whole acre a day. Horse-drawn hay rakes and mechanical reapers were purely experimental technologies in the 1830s, beyond the reach even of progressive farmers. They had, however, adopted one piece of harvesting machinery, the hand-cranked fanning mill, which replaced the winnowing of grain by hand. As grain is fed into this large boxlike machine and the crank is turned, several screens inside shake and separate the grain while a stream of air blows chaff and dirt away. On the Towne Farm, a fanning mill, reproduced for use in winnowing grain, shares a shed room with a great assortment of improved farming implements and utensils.

It was probably the cast-iron plow more than any other mechanical improve-

ment, however, that brought the greatest change to farming in the early nineteenth century. The model patented by John Wood in 1819 gained a wide acceptance in New England. Traditional New England plows had wrought iron shares and wooden moldboards, which were forever clogging up with dirt and weeds. The new plow proved to be much faster and more durable. Its smooth, curving surface—from the tip of the share to the end of the moldboard—turned a furrow over cleanly even in heavy sod. Long waits for repairs at the blacksmith shop were practically eliminated since the cast-iron parts were readily replaceable right on the farm.

The Salem Towne Farm has, in addition to its up-to-date implements, one other feature that marked larger farms in the early nineteenth century: a cider mill. Cider mills were usually owned by well-to-do farmers, and there were no more than four or five in

Opposite: Wearing protective veils and gloves, Village beekeepers hive a swarm of honeybees in the Salem Towne orchard

each community. Now restored as a working exhibit, the horse-powered mill of about 1835 at the Towne Farm was originally located on a farm in Brookfield, New Hampshire.

During most of the year, cider mills like this one stood closed, looking much like any other small barn or shed. But all across New England in September and October, their creaking machinery was hard at work converting most of the region's apple crop to cider. Their horse-powered crushers mashed cartloads of apples for neighborhood farmers, and the great hand-operated screw presses squeezed the juice out through layers of straw or cloth, filling cider barrels for storage at home. "I hope we have enough to make 10 Bbls cider," wrote Thomas Ward of Shrewsbury, Massachusetts, in his journal in the fall of 1831, "if so, we shall do well this season."

For generations, cider, left to turn "hard" or alcoholic, had been New England's daily beverage, drunk by young and old alike. But during the 1830s, cider mills were not quite as busy as they had been earlier. For while some temperance supporters who drew the line at "spirituous liquors" like whiskey and rum thought that moderate consumption of cider was allowable, those who opposed alcohol in any form were gaining strength, and both cider consumption and the acreage of farms planted to orchards were starting to diminish. Progressive farmers, many of whom supported temperance as well as agricultural reform, often found themselves in a quandary. By the 1840s, many of them had closed their cider mills completely.

CHAPTER THREE

Households

THE FAMILY COMPLETELY dominated the ordinary affairs and daily business of rural life in nineteenth-century New England. Not only did New Englanders live together and care for one another in families, they also worked together. Farms, artisans' shops, and stores were invariably managed by families, and their success was often sustained as much by the labor of children as by adults. Sons soon found themselves assisting their fathers, and daughters were introduced early to the endless rounds of their mothers' household duties.

Furthermore, when early New Englanders spoke of their families, they were not only referring to husbands, wives, daughters, and sons, but also to others who might be living in the household. Although it was rare for three complete generations—grandparents, parents, and children—to live together, New England households frequently included other kinfolk or lodgers and workers, such as apprentices, boarding students, hired girls, or farm laborers. Families also commonly made room for relatives or neighbors in need—the handicapped, impoverished, orphaned, widowed, or sick.

Federal census records reveal that throughout the early nineteenth century, the size of New England family households averaged nearly six members, and households of nine or ten were common. In most communities, close to half of the households included at least one member outside the nuclear family; one person in five (one in four in some communities) was an "extra" household member in this sense. Very few Americans lived alone, not only because it was thought to be outrageously peculiar, but also because it was almost impossible to live comfortably outside a working household.

Opposite: Carrying in firewood at the Freeman Farm. New England households consumed enormous quantities of wood, often twenty cords a year

Above: The brightly burning fire in the bake oven will soon become a bed of glowing coals for cooking

49

While family life was thoroughly patriarchal, families were, in many ways, held together by women, whose responsibilities extended from child care to making sure that the members of the household were fed and clothed to income-producing labor. Law and lifeways alike put the husband and father at the head of the family, and, in principle, he governed the household. When she married, a woman's legal identity was joined to that of her husband, and she lost the right she had as a single woman to hold property in her own name. Men claimed at least a supervisory authority over most domestic matters, including the rearing of children and the hiring and management of household help, and it was presumed that they had total control over family finances. Both by custom and in law, fathers had extensive claims to the labor of their children, and account books reveal that wages or credits earned by wives and children were usually recorded in the husband's and father's name as head of the household. In any given family, of course, the strength of an individual personality might have a telling effect, but the force of paternal authority was universally accepted as the norm.

As heads of their households, men also represented their families in the outside world. Only men could vote in elections, hold public office, or serve in the militia. Even though a majority of church members were women, they could not become officers or vote on church affairs. Women were thought to know far less than men about business dealings, legal language, and the close calculation of prices and values.

Although the early nineteenth century was destined to hear some indignant objections to these social arrangements, the dominant view of the period was that men and women were best suited to separate tasks in life. Most women, as well as virtually all men, accepted the notion that the social world was properly divided into two separate spheres of duty and purpose. Each sex possessed, according to its God-given nature, radically differing aptitudes and abilities. Men's roles were public and authoritative, while women's were domestic and subordinate.

Below left: Girls began to learn the domestic arts at an early age, often before seven years old—as here in the kitchen of the Fitch House

Below right: Farm women kept motherhood and child rearing in balance with an enormous variety of tasks

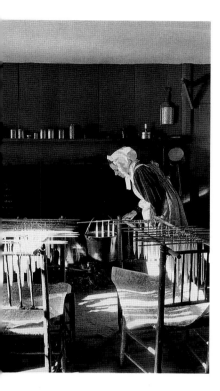

Less romantic than it seems, candle making was in fact a tedious chore. Production of the year's supply of tallow candles is under way in the Freeman kitchen

A woman was expected to find her identity and happiness in family affairs and household responsibilities. Most "female attainments," according to one Connecticut woman, were narrowly confined to "a knowledge of culinary arts and the use of the needle, the loom and the distaff." Such domestic labors were essential for any household to function at all, but they were doubly consequential for any family aspiring to "genteel" standards.

In the countryside more than in the cities, women's domestic responsibilities were both enmeshed with, and distinguished from, the tasks and duties of men. In New England, women did not work in the fields unless the pressure of time was so acute that their labor was absolutely necessary, as with haying or harvest. With rare exceptions, they did not plow, repair tools, stable the cattle, muck out stalls, or go logging in the woods. Instead, their daily realm was centered on the hearth and kitchen and encompassed the house, garden, and farmyard. Women did the cooking, baking, cleaning, washing, and ironing. They tended poultry, made soap and candles, milked cows, churned butter, and pressed cheese.

A country woman's year, on the one hand, followed the cycle of the seasons. After planting gardens and making soap in the springtime, she turned to butter and cheese-making, weeding, and pickling cabbage during the summer. She filled up the root cellar and dried apples and pumpkins in the fall, and salted fresh meats and dipped tallow candles in winter. Her day, on the other hand, was a ceaseless round of chores—preparing meals, washing dishes, washing clothes, sewing, mending, and sweeping up. These tasks were constantly interrupted as she attended to the needs of her children and husband, as well as her wider familial and social obligations.

The job was very difficult to do alone. Daughters began to work alongside their mothers at about age seven. Women with households to run drew on the help of widowed mothers or hired girls, and unmarried sisters, nieces, and cousins often came to stay for weeks or months at a time, helping with housework and children, in a kind of unpaid apprenticeship for a life of domestic labor. From early in the morning until late in the evening, the women worked together to keep the household functioning.

Rural families built up extensive webs of obligation with their neighbors, as they exchanged a great variety of labor and goods—a few days' help in the fields, pasturing for a cow, a load of firewood, the loan of horse and wagon, cheese, or woven cloth. Credits to household accounts were almost always recorded in the name of the man, but much of what a farm family could offer in trade was actually produced by the women and girls. Women brought quantities of cheese, butter, eggs, knitted socks, and even beeswax and feathers to country stores, taking credits and manufactured or imported goods in exchange.

As her labor was considered a family resource, a young woman might spend a few days a week spinning or dairying for a nearby household as part of her family's balance of credits and debits. Susan Blunt of Merrimack, New Hampshire, was ten years old when she was borrowed by a neighboring family to keep house for a week for small twin girls and their invalid grandfather. Having been told to "work like a little spider," she hauled water, cooked breakfast and dinner, got the girls off to school, and baked biscuits. She was permitted to keep the pay she received for such a remarkable demonstration of

domestic capability, and with it she bought herself a new calico apron.

In addition to tending to the daily needs of households, women, of course, were primarily responsible for clothing their families as well. Throughout the eighteenth century, household textiles and clothing were produced in staggering quantities at home. Indeed, the domestic task of preparing and spinning flax and wool had occupied so much time that the word "spinster" came to symbolize the role of single women. At the opening of the nineteenth century, nearly all women in country neighborhoods could spin yarn, although handloom weaving was the province of those with greater skill. But by the 1820s and 1830s, factory-made textiles were widely available, and most women of southern and central New England were ceasing to spin and weave at home.

Clothing was traditionally costly, whether calculated by unending home labor or hard-won dollars, and most people owned relatively few garments. About 1800, a typical country housewife might have no more than two or three dresses, with one saved as a "best Sunday" gown. Men and boys commonly owned two sets of clothes—shirt, vest, trousers, and long homespun frock—with one in coarse linen, or "towcloth," for the summer and another in wool for winter. Before ready-made shoe production accelerated in the 1820s, children in middling families and even some adults in poorer ones went barefoot in the summer. Although the production of fabric and the cut of clothes altered greatly during the early nineteenth century, folks living in areas far from stores and the growing commercial economy dressed in "homespun" linen or wool for many years.

Families in far northern New England still produced many of their own fabrics in the 1830s, and Nathaniel Hawthorne noted in his travel journals how often he came across people wearing homespun clothing in the hills of Vermont and central Maine.

New England's Industrial Revolution carried many rural women and children away to factories and brought a flood of "outwork" opportunities to the many thousands more who stayed at home. These were tasks that women could pick up intermittently along with the usual chores of domestic work; in many New England families, they simply took over the time that had previously been devoted to home spinning and weaving.

In the face of these changes, the old boundaries between male and female roles persisted. In many respects, women continued to work within the context of their traditional métier: their handwork for industries was heavily concentrated on tasks involving sewing, textile production, weaving, painting, and decorating, which were not considered to be "men's work." Even where men and women worked in the same industries, they almost always used different skills or tools and performed different parts of a process; far more women brought the work home than ever boarded at the mills or labored in shops. Wages for women still reflected their economic subordination and were lower by one-half or two-thirds than the rates paid to men.

The nation's earliest full-scale industrial survey was undertaken in 1832 under the direction of the secretary of the treasury, and its schedules were particularly detailed for the communities of rural New England. Louis McLane's report recorded that more than seven thousand women—or about half of all women under thirty—were at work for wages in Worcester County, Massachusetts. Slightly more than one-third of them were working in the mechanized production of textiles: about 1,750 in cotton factories and more than 640 at woolen mills.

A greater number of these working women, almost three-fifths, were busy at occupations that could be carried on part-time at home. More than twenty-five hundred women and girls were making palm-leaf hats out of materials brought in from Central America, more than one thousand were employed at braiding straw and making straw hats, and some five hundred were binding and stitching shoe uppers. Women and girls worked on shoes sometimes alongside their fathers and brothers. Straw braiders and palm-leaf workers were employed by country storekeepers who organized the trade and advertised in local newspapers for women to work in exchange for credit and attractive consumer goods.

Smaller numbers of working women were scattered throughout a multitude of lesser industries in Worcester County: polishing combs, bottoming chairs, painting on toys and tinware, bookbinding, and making twine and wicking. There were also women working unrecorded by the survey as domestic "helps" in households, teaching school for three or four months a year, and working in the "needle trades"—arts too feminine to be classified as "industries." All told they amounted to about one-third of the female population over fourteen years old.

Most of them were young and unmarried. The great majority of women in their late twenties and over thirty could be found managing their households as farm or village wives, or were widows with their own responsibilities.

At Old Sturbridge Village, working households exhibit the changing ways women contributed to the economy of their families in the 1830s. Family and work remain integrated in the Freeman Farmhouse, the most self-sufficient among them as regards the necessities of life. At the Bixby House, home of a rural artisan/farmer's family, new kinds of household production have been taken up to provide a modest measure of prosperity. And the ways found by widowed or unmarried women to live independently are explored at the Fenno House in the center village.

The Freeman Farmhouse

The modest one-and-a-half-story gambrel-roofed house built by a local housewright between 1810 and 1815 that is now the centerpiece of the Freeman Farm at Old Sturbridge Village was home for Pliny and Delia Freeman of Sturbridge, Massachusetts, and several of their children and kin beginning in 1828. Archaeological studies of the original site a couple of miles southeast of the museum reveal that the main part of the present kitchen ell was added to the house shortly after the Freemans moved in. The new space included a cooking hearth and bake oven, along with an unheated room, all conveniently distinct from the front of the house. Later, the Freemans extended the ell to create other working spaces, including a dairy, completing a service wing well-suited to the doings of a busy household.

The kitchen fireplace was the hub of the early-nineteenth-century home, and the farm woman's first chore in the morning was to tend to it. Usually, there were a few embers "banked" from the night before; if not, it was necessary to strike a fire with flint and steel or send to the neighbors' for hot coals. Cooking fireplaces were hung with swinging iron "cranes" that held large pots and kettles over the fire, but much cooking was also done in footed iron skillets or pots placed over small beds of glowing coals. The cooking fires and centuries-old hearth-cooking skills have been rekindled at the Freeman Farmhouse, where interpreters prepare meals daily and bake every week.

One baking day each week was enough for most families, although large households might fire their ovens more often. Like most brick bake ovens, the one at the farmhouse is about three feet deep, built into the wall of the fireplace. A small fire is built directly inside the oven to heat it. When the flame has burned down and the hot coals emptied out, the cook may test the temperature by throwing in a little flour to see how quickly it browns. Or she may follow the example of Mary Livermore, a young Charlestown, Massachusetts, housewife, who learned how her mother-in-law "would hold her hand in the oven till she could count twenty." As soon as the heat is right, breads, pies, puddings, and cakes are slipped into the hot oven on a long-handled iron peel. One of the breads often baked in the Freeman oven is made from a recipe, or "receipt," that appeared in a popular 1830s book of practical household advice. In *The American Frugal Housewife*, Lydia Maria Child declared that "some think the nicest of all bread is one third Indian [cornmeal], one third rye, and one third flour, made according

Overleaf: The Freeman House—painted a distinctive early-nineteenth-century shade of red—as seen from the garden fence

to the directions for flour bread." The rye and corn are grown on the farm and ground at the nearby Gristmill. But the wheat flour must be purchased at the store today, just as it would have been in the 1830s.

Productive farming families of the 1830s relied on their own produce for most of their food supplies. With credits earned by selling butter and cheese to the local store, they might purchase coffee, tea, sugar, salt, molasses, spices, and the occasional barrel of flour. But almost everything else could be produced at home or obtained through exchanges with neighboring families. Lyndon Freeman, Pliny's nephew, recalled that by early winter most farmsteads had "at least a pork and beef of sufficient quantity," and a larder "well supplied with butter, cheese, applesauce, pickles, sausages, souse, etc." Large quantities of food were kept on hand in country homes, and the women at the Freeman Farmhouse spend countless hours producing, procuring, and processing staple foodstuffs.

From the windows of the kitchen, women of the household kept a mindful eye on their gardens. The Freeman kitchen garden—tightly fenced to keep out "vermin"— fills a full quarter acre, just right for the needs of a family of eight to ten. Kitchen gardens were tended for the most part by women and children, save for a spring plowing and harrowing that required a man and a team of oxen. Fresh greens, peas, peppers, and "cowcumbers" were welcome summer fare. Onions and other root crops, squashes, cabbages, and beans were sometimes eaten freshly picked, but also were grown in large quantities for winter storage. Many garden vegetables were stored in root cellars or garrets after harvest in the fall. Turnips, parsnips, and carrots were kept in bins of sand, while winter squashes, cabbages, ears of seed corn, bunches of herbs, shell beans, and peas were hung up to dry. Visitors to the farmhouse may find interpreters drying pumpkins, salting down pork, or pickling beets and cabbage. Apples are stored whole and used for cider. Hours of work go into paring apples and boiling down the sweet "cider molasses" needed to make applesauce.

The root cellar's array of winter-keeping vegetables—pumpkins, winter squash, cabbage, and onions

The smokehouse on the Freeman Farm

Even though garden seeds were commercially available from the Shakers as well as more worldly horticulturists by the 1830s, many gardeners—and farmers as well—continued to raise much of their own seed. For beans, peas, and corn the process is as simple as setting aside a small portion of the crop being dried for winter storage. But for other vegetables, one or two plants of each type must be left unharvested in the garden until they flower and set seeds in the fall. Biennials, like carrots, turnips, and beets, will yield seeds only if some choice samples are selected from the root cellar and planted again in early spring. Once the mature seeds have been harvested and cleaned, they can be tucked away in folded paper packets or hand-stitched envelopes until the following year. Today, women at the Freeman household grow heirloom varieties, such as "Boston Marrow" squash or "Early Horn" and "Long Orange" carrots. Just as farmers save the finest ears of Rhode Island flint corn to seed their cornfields, gardeners use their own seed to plant such old-fashioned beans as White Dutch runners, caseknife, and cranberry red.

Francis Underwood, remembering his hometown of Enfield, Massachusetts, in the 1830s, said that few farming households "had regular supplies of fresh meat. Except at the autumnal pig-killing, or at the slaughter of a lamb in the spring, or very rarely in winter of a steer, their tables were furnished with salted beef and pork from their own cellar, and with dried salt fish." The butchering of a pig, a lamb, or a cow is an enormous amount of work for both the men and women at the Freeman Farm. Large kettles and tubs for scalding are needed, as well as containers for salting and for storage. For several days, the women are busy preparing meat, cleaning tripe, rendering tallow, and making sausage. Since this is almost always a winter chore, some of the meat is stored in an unheated attic or lean-to, some is brined for storage in the cellar, and some is inevitably "borrowed" by neighbors, to be repaid when they do their own butchering. Hams are salted down to be smoked in the smokehouse by the garden.

Although most farm products were regularly used as items of exchange with neighbors, a well-managed dairy was the farming household's most reliable economic link with the world outside the neighborhood. Butter and cheese, for which there was a ready market in fast-growing cities and villages, were, along with hay, New England's real "cash crops," far more important than bread grains. Dairying brought small gains to marginal farm families, a measure of prosperity for farmers of the "middling sort," and wealth to a few. One or two cows would supply the milk needed by a family, but it took three or four to provide surplus enough for market. Cheese was more easily made during the warm summer months, and butter in the cooler days of spring and fall. The balance of production between longer-keeping cheese and more perishable butter was usually determined by how distant a farm was from its principal market. No matter what the product, the work was, and is today, relentless.

The cows are milked—in New England, this was women's work—at the barn twice each day, and the fresh milk is brought to the dairy at the Freeman Farmhouse. The milk is then strained through fine cloth into shallow pans of tin or redware—1830s dairywomen used both—and set aside in a cool place for at least twenty-four hours. By then, the cream has risen enough that it can be skimmed off the top and set aside to ripen. The interpreters at the Freeman Farm say that slightly soured cream is best for making butter, which many households did twice a week. By whipping the dasher vigorously

Opposite: A quiet, sunlit moment in the Freeman House

Right: In the Freeman kitchen, signs of a bountiful harvest, and the unceasing labor of food preparation

in a simple upright churn, usually for an hour or so, dairywomen bring the cream—almost mysteriously—to butter. Then they "work" the butter, cleaning it in cold water and kneading and pressing it into a firm consistency. When it is ready, the butter is packed with salt to preserve it and sealed for storage or shipment in stoneware crocks or oak tubs. Producing a clean, flavorful, long-lasting butter requires dexterity, strength, and judgment.

Traditionally, dairying is dependent on the seasons and can only begin after spring pasturing and the freshening of cattle. Cheesemaking also requires the butchering of a calf. The calf's stomach, or "maw," is salted and stretched out to dry for use throughout the season. Soaking it in brine yields rennet, the source of a digestive enzyme crucial to the process. At least twice a week at the Freeman Farmhouse in summer, milk is warmed in a large brass kettle and rennet is added to curdle the milk for making cheese. Once the curd has formed, it is cut into small squares so the watery milk, or whey, can be ladled off and heated. After the curd has been scalded in the hot liquid to force out more whey, the dairywoman drains the curd and places it in a cloth-lined hoop for pressing. The curd is squeezed in a wooden cheese press for several hours to remove the excess whey and moisture, then turned and pressed again. Finished cheeses are set on the upper shelves of the dairy to age and are regularly turned and rubbed with fat. A thin rind forms, which preserves the moisture content and protects the cheese from flies. Within a couple of months cheese develops sufficient flavor to be consumed. In the 1830s the cheeses were kept until needed at the family table or gathered up to take to the store.

When Pliny Freeman added a new service wing to the house, he was clearly investing in his family's growing capacity for profitable household work. At the same time, however, he closed off an outside doorway and moved some stairs to make a new "best room," or parlor, as an improved and more private space for the family. Thanks to dirt roads, nearby barnyards, and open fireplaces, virtually all nineteenth-century farmhouses were dirty and dusty. There were no window screens, so every room was full of flies all summer and flyspecks soiled the walls and furnishings. Yet, away from the heat of the cooking hearth and the bustling routines of the dairy, the new room brought a fresh dimension of comfortable living to the family. Although it may seem decidedly plain and spare to today's visitors, it was a quiet refuge where a woman might spend the afternoon sewing, knitting, entertaining callers, writing letters to her kinfolk, or enjoying a moment of rest.

Pliny Freeman's farm and family evidently went through difficult years that coincided with the declining health of his wife Delia, who fell seriously ill in 1836. Previously, he had kept a horse, a team of oxen, four cows, several young cattle, one pig, and about twenty-five sheep. But in that year, he sold off most of his sheep and all but one of the cows: there was no one at home who could tend the dairy. Pliny took work as a housewright until "hay time," and his teenage daughter went to live with one of her married sisters. His seventeen-year-old son stayed on to work the farm.

Deprived of the labor of women, households in early New England literally fell apart. Only the year before, Pliny and Delia had been caring for an infant grandson,

Opposite: *The cream is skimmed from a pan of fresh milk, then set aside for butter making*

Left: A patent cheese press and a "rocking" butter churn, both devices that sought to make dairying more efficient

whose mother, their eldest daughter, had been killed freakishly by a bolt of lightning. Pliny wrote to another son living in Ohio that the grieving son-in-law had "stopped housekeeping and will hire his board."

In 1839, Delia died of "consumption," or tuberculosis. Following hard upon Pliny's sorrow was the pressing need to locate someone—whether it be a daughter, a wife, or hired help—who could keep his house, and he wrote to his family sharing his grief and revealing his worry over "how to calculate about a housekeeper." Son Dwight and daughter Augusta dutifully returned from an extended journey to Ohio to help their grieving father on the farm and to keep his house. Work continued on modest improvements around the farmstead, and some of it must have been finished late in 1839. The following February, the widow Mary Pease wrote to congratulate Pliny: "I was glad to hear you have got your house painted and a dooryard." Both these efforts were major steps in the history of rural improvement, and Pliny must have been greatly pleased when, later that year, Mary wrote again to accept his proposal to marry.

The Bixby House

Emerson and Laura Bixby were newly married in 1823 when they set up housekeeping in an outlying neighborhood of Barre, Massachusetts, called Four Corners. About thirty miles north of Sturbridge, it was one of the many country neighborhoods—small clusters of dwellings, farms, and shops—that dotted the New England landscape. Families living in such places responded more slowly to changing times than did their counterparts in cities or center villages. But, as the Bixbys demonstrate, they too reshaped their lives.

Emerson Bixby came to Four Corners to work as a blacksmith for a wagon-and-sleigh maker. He then purchased a small lot for his own blacksmith shop across the road and a little later bought the house and barn on a one-and-a-half-acre parcel next to the wagon shop. There, near the homestead farms of Emerson's parents, grandparents, and uncles, the couple raised three daughters and sought to bring some measure of "the new" gentility to the traditional ways of the countryside. The Bixbys did not leave behind letters or diaries to document their personal lives. But Emerson Bixby's account book survived, and this, along with the museum's exhaustive archaeological, architectural, and documentary study of the Four Corners property and neighborhood, provides insight into the family's world.

Living on a smaller parcel of land, Laura Bixby and her three daughters did less farmwork than the Freeman women, instead contributing to the household in different ways. Clues from business records suggest that Laura Bixby as a young wife sewed shoe uppers—this was called "fitting" or "binding" work—for a shoemaker across the road, probably earning between three and five cents per pair. By the late 1830s and 1840s, the Bixby girls were entering their teenage years and their work became increasingly valuable to the family. The account book suggests that they were helping their mother braid

The Emerson Bixby House, with doors and shutters of bright Paris green. Its front yard, characteristic of the New England countryside, is rough and unfinished

straw and make palm-leaf hats for a storekeeper in Barre's center village, and the material record bears this out; scraps of shoe leather, palm-leaf trimmings, and pieces of straw braid have all been found beneath the floorboards of the house. Study of the house indicates that the Bixbys added a dairy or cheese room to the house during this period as well.

At the Bixby House today, visitors can watch interpreters bind shoes and braid straw when they are not occupied by their other household chores. Sitting near a window for the light, the binder bends closely over her work. With an awl she swiftly punches holes in the thin pieces of leather, cut to patterned shapes, that are held between her knees in a simple wooden clamp. Through these holes go needles or stiff hog's-hair "bristles," attached to both ends of a hand-twisted linen cord that she nimbly manipulates along with the awl. She binds the side seams with a "double-running" stitch, closes the backs with a "butt stitch," sews in the heel-stiffening counters with a "whip stitch," and uses a basting stitch to put in linings of calfskin or linen. On the floor beside her is a basket full of leather parts and simple tools—a marking wheel, shoe knives, beeswax, and a ball of linen thread.

The craft of braiding straw also requires manual dexterity. The rye straw is cut green for braiding, then scalded in hot water, and put out to bleach in the sun. (Scotsman Patrick Shirreff, traveling through New England in 1835, found "innumerable bundles of rye straw . . . bleaching around the cottages.") The braider pulls any remaining leaves off the dry straw and cuts straight pieces from the jointed stems. She then dampens the straw, slits it open, flattens it, and pulls it through the tiny teeth of a hand-held splitting tool to produce strips of straw ready to braid. In Laura Bixby's day, all braiders had at least to master the seven-strand and the eleven-strand patterns that made the familiar Dunstable and Leghorn weaves. Braiding was, and still is, tiresome work, but it easily turned women's spare time into paid time.

Along with new opportunities for outwork, the traditional routines of country life prevail in the Bixby House at the Village. In winter, the women make a year's supply of candles by tying short pieces of braided cotton wicking to slender rods and repeatedly dipping the hanging wicks into a cauldron of melted suet of beef or mutton, called tallow. As in most farm households, they make good soap in the spring or fall by boiling animal fat and a little lye, made from hardwood ashes. They cultivate a traditional assortment of vegetables and a few common ornamentals—sunflowers, hollyhocks, and four o'clocks—for their enjoyment in a small, fenced kitchen garden, but only tend them as time allows.

For the first decade or so after the Bixbys moved into the small three-room house, they made few changes. Cramped and dark by our standards, the house, with its unpainted clapboards, off-center chimney stack, and asymmetrical layout was typical of the local countryside. Following traditional New England practice, the wallpapered "best room" was used for entertaining visitors, for family dining and washing dishes, and even as a bedroom for the parents. Most domestic work was done in the dark-red kitchen and in a small sitting room, whose carelessly hung wallpaper and use of paint to imitate decorative woodwork spoke of "rustic" taste. The children slept in the unfinished and unheated attic. Ashes, trash, and broken dishes accumulated in the yard. With no entry hall to ensure privacy, visitors entered directly into the living quarters.

Starting in the late 1830s, as the three girls grew older and the family was earning more money, there was a burst of improvement. Ceilings were plastered, closets finished, and the house was given its first coat of exterior paint—a fashionable white. Dark walls were lightened with new wallpaper and paint. The house itself was enlarged, giving it a greater sense of fashionable symmetry: the new wing off the kitchen included a separate bedroom for Emerson and Laura and a bedchamber above it for the girls, as well as a private entranceway, making it possible to close off the exterior doors to the kitchen and best room. A small dairy room was also built in the new wing, which, along with the family's earlier acquisition of thirty-two acres of nearby farmland, reflected the growing importance of dairying to the household economy.

This flurry of spending provides a vivid example of the transforming effects of a changing economy and new ideals of domestic order. Families like the Bixbys and the

A reproduction wooden pump brings fresh water into the sink in the Bixby House ell. On its original site in Barre, Massachusetts, the ell was built over a dug well

Below: Braiding straw occupied the available time of many thousands of New England women and girls in the 1830s

Bottom: Bundles of sun-bleached rye straw, along with handheld splitting tools, rest atop a partly finished straw hat. Below are examples of the weaving patterns that braiders needed to master

Right: On the "home lot" of the Bixby House, a reproduced early-nineteenth-century privy. In traditional rural style, it is highly visible and situated disconcertingly close to the hog pen

Left: This wooden rocker, a long-time possession of the Bixby family, was clearly upholstered at home. It is an attempt to turn an ordinary slat-back chair into a piece of fashionable furniture

Opposite: The "best room" at the Bixby House. In the most traditional rural households, the parents' canopied bed shared pride of place with parlor furnishings

Freemans in outlying neighborhoods would lag behind those in the bustling center villages, but they too eventually accepted change on their own terms. The Bixbys never did acquire the latest household goods in fashion—cookstoves, parlor carpets, and sofas—but their accomplishments with relatively slender means were nonetheless impressive. By combining income from blacksmithing with part-time farming and outwork, this working family achieved a comfortable sufficiency, moving farther away from old country ways and toward new standards of domestic abundance and order.

The Fenno House and Barn. This house remains unpainted, as were some traditional homes even into the 1830s

The Fenno House

Only a few flowering bushes and some old-fashioned perennial plants adorn the casually tended dooryard at the Fenno House. Weeds and woodchips gather around the pathways that cross between the house, its nearby barn, and the privy. Unlike the other houses facing the Village Common, this one remains unpainted, its clapboard siding dark and weather-beaten. With a central but slightly asymmetrical chimney and small entryway, kitchen and parlor on the ground floor, and two chambers above, it is a good example of a traditional New England "hall-parlor" house. Originally built in Canton, Massachusetts, about fifteen miles south of Boston, the 1704 house is the oldest dwelling at the museum, and it depicts a way of life that even in the 1830s would have been behind the times.

The Fenno House interprets daily life as a composite image, drawing upon many historical sources and abundant research to portray the home of an elderly widow and her unmarried daughter. In this house, the War of Independence itself and the tumultuous changes that followed it are well remembered. Most of the furnishings in the house date back before 1800, and even some to the years before the Revolution.

In a society in which many women were widowed early and some never married, nearly one household in ten in rural communities was headed by a woman. In fact, the number both of widows who never remarried and of spinsters was increasing in New England during the early nineteenth century. Newer settlements to the West drew disproportionally on young unmarried men, leaving an increasing number of women behind who needed to find sustaining economic and social roles in their communities. Most often, they discovered opportunities in the traditional skills of their familiar domain: managing a household, taking in boarders, making textiles, or working in the various needle trades. Sewing was a skill that virtually every New England woman learned as a young girl. A woman with first-rate skills and an eye for fashion could set up in business with little capital investment.

The right of dower, part of the English common law that had been defined by statute across the New England states, was essential to the support of widows. It gave a widow the uncontested right during her lifetime to one-third of the real property owned by her husband. She was entitled to the property even in cases of insolvency, and her "widow's third" was paid before obligations to any creditors. Husbands who wrote wills could leave their widows a larger share of property, or on different terms, but often did not. The law assumed and custom decreed that a widow should have ample support

The Fenno House parlor

Right: A rare early-nineteenth-century depiction of a rural household's interior. An elderly woman can be seen reading while a toddler crawls in the foreground (Oil painting, Interior of Jennings Homestead by Marcia Ann Kilbourn, c. 1845)

Opposite: Taking a moment from work to savor the blooms in the Fenno House dooryard

during her lifetime, but that full ownership of property would pass on to children or grandchildren after her death.

The legal record of inheritance shows that the provision of the widow's third could become a difficult and intricate process, particularly if married children were to share the farmstead and house with their mother. One Leicester, Massachusetts, widow was given a sitting room and bedchamber, along with the "privilege to pass to and from said rooms through kitchen and front door. Also privilege in the kitchen to wash, bake and to do other work which cannot be done in the southwest room." Along with this went use of the well, cellar space for storing garden crops, and a place in the yard for her firewood. Some widows lived comfortably with a married child and family under such arrangements, while others found them occasions for quarreling and difficulty. The women who counted themselves most fortunate were those who did not have to share their dwellings at all, because their children and grandchildren had consented to "leaving mother on the homestead."

At the Fenno House, the village portrays two independent-minded women who exchange yarn and woven cloth, occasionally house a boarder, and rent out fields and pasture to earn a respectable, though none-too-generous, income. With its animals in the barnyard and a large fenced garden out back, the Fenno House also has an ongoing involvement in small-scale farming.

Even though the availability of factory-made textiles by the 1830s had finally silenced the wheels and looms in most rural homes, some practitioners of the old art carried on. One of them, Sarah Bryant of Cummington, Massachusetts, increased her weaving after her husband died in 1820 and their eldest son took charge of the farm. Her diary entries describe an astonishing variety of projects, from bed ticks, "homespun plaid," and shirting to cheesecloth, "fine flannel," and warp-striped carpets.

Winter light outlines the frame and harnesses of the loom. The shuttle rests on top of a piece of weaving already well underway

The Barrett household of New Hartford, Connecticut, was also one of single women living without men. As Samantha Barrett's diary describes it, she and her sister Zeloda never married, staying on with their widowed mother to keep the small family homestead together. The women maintained a garden, kept cows, and raised sheep; they hired men and boys from the neighborhood to help with chores like plowing, fence repair, and shoveling manure, and paid them in kind. They took their own wool to the carding mill and did their own spinning at home, and although Samantha passed her evenings knitting stockings for sale, the main source of the family's income came from her weaving. She spent all or part of every day at the loom. In 1828, along with nineteen yards of rag carpeting for use at home, she produced over four hundred yards of woolen cloth for her customers. She often used her own homespun thread, and many of her customers brought their own wool to be made into fabric or blankets.

In the small spaces of the Fenno House room is found for the spinning wheel and the heavy wooden loom, with its shuttles, quills, weights, and reeds. Manufactured cotton and woolen cloth filled most of the needs of the countryside by the 1830s, but useful niches remained for spinning and weaving. Some women both old and young continued to use their spinning wheels to produce yarn for knitting stockings, scarves, and mittens, or for their own weaving. In the Fenno House, wool is spun on a walking or "great" wheel, reproduced from an example in the museum's collections. One reminiscing New Englander recalled the grace that spinning required: "a free movement of the arms, an elastic pose, and a long gliding step, advancing and retreating. The country people said there was a knack to it."

Some skilled handloom weavers continued to find local customers for their blankets, simple carpets, coverlets, and specialty fabrics. The loom is a heavy wooden frame whose treadle-operated harnesses hold the hundreds of threads of the "warp" in a complex array set up by the weaver. As the weaver works, she uses the foot treadles in a complicated, repeating sequence to raise and lower various sets of warp threads on the loom. Then, back and forth through the opening and closing rows of warp, she passes the shuttle carrying the weft thread. With a practiced and rhythmic coordination of eyes, hands, and feet, she throws and catches the wooden shuttle, pulls a "beater" sharply forward to press the filling thread into the warp, and checks to keep her edges even.

The fabrics that visitors can see on Village looms are highly accurate reproductions for use and display. Because antique textiles are extremely fragile, subject to fading and deterioration from sunlight, and can only be displayed for brief periods of time, the reproductions are vital to the museum's exhibits. They are copied from textiles in the collection or based on early-nineteenth-century patterns called "weavers' drafts." Village farmers wear woolen frocks made from cloth that has been grown, spun, and woven at the museum, as are the plaid or checkered kerchiefs around their necks. Beds in the households are covered with Village-woven blankets in traditional solid colors or bright stripes and plaids.

The bedchamber over the parlor of the Fenno House is furnished to be shared by the women, a sleeping arrangement typical of the early nineteenth century. During warm weather, it is also a place for sewing. The kitchen chamber is furnished for a boarder, reflecting another way in which women on their own made ends meet. "My boarding place is as good as I need," wrote a young schoolteacher in his diary. "It is with an old lady of 70 years and her daughter a widow of 45 perhaps." A boarder paid a fee in cash or credit, usually between one and two dollars a week, for which he received room, board, and laundry. Very often, boarders were young men just starting out in life away from home: journeymen, clerks, or teachers. A young store clerk or shoemaker would spend little time in his room, working six long days a week, and often returning to the shop or store after the evening meal. If his family lived nearby, a boarder might travel home for a visit on the Sabbath. The women living in a household like this one might

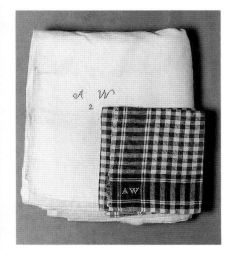

"Handkerchiefs" in the early nineteenth century were squares of cloth that men tied around their necks and women draped over their shoulders. These early examples are marked with the owner's initials

Overleaf: A view of the Center Village outskirts, showing the back lots and outbuildings of the Fitch and Fenno Houses

Opposite: *Spinning wool on the "great wheel" or "walking wheel"*

have seen little of their boarder, but his presence bolstered their household economy and helped them remain independent.

The Herb Garden

Although some were surely far more expert than others, virtually every rural housewife knew something of herbs and their uses. The Herb Garden displays the Village's extensive collection of over four hundred plants that early New Englanders cultivated for medicinal use, fragrance, or flavoring. With systematically arranged arrays of labeled specimens, it is virtually a living encyclopedia. Many of the varieties grown here can also be found in the kitchen and dooryard gardens of the Village's houses. The Herb Garden is laid out on a gentle slope, with paths winding through three levels of raised beds. Native wild varieties and generally useful household plants are on the upper level, culinary herbs in the central section, and medicinal plants at the bottom. There are small sample plantings of crops once grown commercially for the textile industry, including teasels for combing wool and unusual dye plants such as woad. Several plants displayed—such as joe-pye weed, goldenrod, loosestrife, poke, toadflax, and even dandelions—are considered weeds today, but had a wide variety of uses in the past.

Popular culinary or pot herbs grown in early New England gardens included the familiar sage, summer savory, sweet marjoram, basil, mint, and thyme. However, they shared space with many varieties less well known today, such as angelica, fenugreek, chervil, and flagroot. Aromatic herbs were used to produce sweet sachets, potpourris, scented lotions, and moth preventatives, and the garden includes a section devoted to them, including scented geraniums, southernwood, myrtle, clove pink, and santolina.

The herbal lore of the British Isles, with significant additions from Native American traditions, was remembered in every New England household. Formally trained physicians, practitioners of "botanic" Thompsonian medicine and other eclectic therapies, African-American and Native American herb doctors and "doctresses," and family healers all used medicinal plants, or "simples," as remedies for common ills and injuries. Herbal teas and brews, plasters and compresses, liniments and tinctures were used to treat ailments ranging from fevers and burns to rheumatism. Strong teas of thoroughwort, succory, pennyroyal, and tansy were recommended as remedies for digestive disorders. Coughs might be soothed with a tea of coltsfoot and flaxseed, fevers eased by sweet balm or catnip. A poultice of chickweed was thought to relieve a toothache, and balms of wormwood or Gilead buds were used to heal wounds. Although many herbal therapies have been supplanted with the emergence of modern medical science, curative properties have been confirmed in dozens of plants, including foxglove, belladonna, valerian root, and henbane. Plant substances remain the basis for a very large portion of medications in use today, and there has been a revival of interest in the traditional uses of herbs. The Herb Garden presents and preserves a living horticultural collection of enduring significance.

Overleaf: *The Herb Garden, an extensive living collection of early New England's useful plants*

CHAPTER FOUR

The Mill Neighborhood

Opposite: A winter view of the Village Millpond and covered bridge

Above: One of the "carding engines" at the Carding Mill.

Overleaf: The Mill Neighborhood. In the foreground are the Bixby House and the Blacksmith Shop. The Carding Mill and Sawmill are in the background

NEW ENGLAND'S TOPOGRAPHY PROVIDES THOUsands of small waterpower sites, and mills were among the very earliest enterprises to appear throughout the region because they were indispensable to farming and building. By the early nineteenth century most farmers were within easy hauling distance of the waterwheels that drove small-scale mills for grinding grain, sawing lumber, "fulling" handwoven cloth, or "carding" wool for spinning. Country mills were built just about everywhere a river or stream could be made to drop a few feet—by damming, dredging, digging, and building flumes and raceways. Very commonly, the mills were owned by prosperous neighborhood farmers, who were paid for their services with tolls taken from the grist or with goods and work, rather than with cash.

How such small mills once harnessed the power of falling water can be seen today at Old Sturbridge Village, where a sawmill, gristmill, and carding mill have been "seated" on the millpond. Nearby is the shop and home of a blacksmith. The growth of mill neighborhoods in the early nineteenth century paralleled the rise of the center villages and represented part of the industrialization of the countryside. By the 1830s, sizable textile manufactures—factory buildings of two or three stories—had been constructed at the best sites, and another kind of village started to grow up around them. Two- and four-family houses, more artisans' shops, and company-owned stores soon characterized the early mill villages of the Industrial Revolution. But across the countryside the smaller sites with their neighborhood service mills remained.

The waterpowered saw is captured in
mid-cut. The heavy log carriage, governed by the geared wheel at right,
advances the log into the blade

Sawmill

Sometime early in the 1790s, a Sturbridge farmer named David Wight, Jr., diverted the
Quinebaug River to develop a millpond site and build a sawmill. A nineteenth-century
historian described, and Old Sturbridge Village archaeologists later confirmed, how he

"dug through the sandbank and made a canal" to create a pond. He then dammed the pond to gain a head of water that would turn his wheel, and dug out a channel below "to conduct the water away down through the meadow to the river again." The water still flows through Wight's millpond, but before the property became part of the site of Old Sturbridge Village, all his buildings had long since disappeared. New England's rural mills, mechanical marvels in their own time, were eventually undone by the insistent progress of technology. As steam power and faster transportation arrived, and the rural economy shrank, the small mills of the eighteenth and nineteenth centuries were gradually abandoned. Very few of them have survived to the present, except for the remains of their stone dams and foundations scattered across the countryside. Those lost technologies have been restored and re-created at Old Sturbridge Village, where Wight's old millpond echoes once again with the creaking wheels, whirling gears, and thumping saw frames of a working mill neighborhood.

Sawmills of the centuries-old "up-and-down" design had once been common in every New England town—Sturbridge alone accounted for thirteen in 1831. Yet virtually all reciprocating saws were replaced by more efficient circular ones in the decades after 1840, and traditional waterwheels and transmission systems began to disappear soon after. The Village's extensive search for an early mill in working order was unsuccessful. Probably the longest-surviving mill with an up-and-down mechanism was the Nichols-Colby Sawmill of Bow, New Hampshire, which was destroyed in the hurricane of 1938. Fortunately, meticulous architectural drawings of the mill had been completed by the Historic American Building Survey only the year before. Using this detailed documentation and the staff's extensive research into mill technology, the museum built a sawmill and brought to life a working world known only through fragmentary accounts and archaeological study.

The Sawmill, like most in the early nineteenth century, is situated downstream of the dam. It is a long, narrow structure with an ell attached, all heavily framed with massive timbers, tightly joined and well braced. The sides of the building are left open so that logs can be rolled in on one side and sawn lumber skidded down the steeply angled poles on the other. A pair of cast-iron tracks runs the length of the sawing floor to guide a mechanized carriage, which feeds the logs through the saw. Two heavy "fender posts" stand upright, framed into the center of the mill, flanking the carriage. The fender posts are grooved to receive a wooden saw frame, or sash, which slides up and down, carrying a tightly mounted saw blade six or seven feet long and about eight inches wide.

When the gate in the dam is opened, water comes rushing through the wooden flume and drops into an iron sluice, or "penstock," where it whirls through the twin turbines that provide power to the machinery. These two cast-iron "reaction wheels," reconstructed from a U.S. patent given to Calvin Wing of Vermont in 1820, spin at high speed in reaction to the powerful jets of water being squirted through their six nozzles. Heavy wooden rods, called "pitmans" because they replace the bottom sawyer, or "pit man," in traditional hand sawing, connect the cranks on the wheel shafts to the saw frame above, and carry the powerful motion of the waterwheels to the saw. At the rate of about eighty to ninety strokes per minute, the saw is driven up and down with a loud, pounding cadence that can be heard throughout the neighborhood. A ratchet system with a

The Sawmill and the sawmill dam.
Sawn lumber is skidded down the poles
to be stacked in the yard on the near side
of the mill

rack-and-pinion gear moves the log-bearing carriage slightly forward with each raising of the saw frame, pulling the log into the saw blade, which cuts on the downstroke. To avoid sawing into the carriage, each cut must be stopped a few inches from the end of the log, and the carriage is returned to begin the next cut by engaging a separate, smaller waterwheel. When all the cuts are made in the log, it is rolled off the carriage, and the newly sawed boards are split off from the unsawed stump.

The "stub shot," or short split end of each board, is a characteristic feature—along with the distinctive linear sawmarks—of lumber produced in an up-and-down sawmill. Small circular blades are used in the two small waterpowered bench saws in the ell at the Sawmill. One, a cutoff saw, is used to trim boards to length, and the other, a ripsaw, cuts them to any variety of specified widths. By the early 1800s small circular saws like these were increasingly common, but rotary blades large enough to saw whole logs eluded mechanics and ironworkers until later in the century.

Running a sawmill was rarely a full-time occupation. Water flow was seasonal, and mills had only local markets since logs and lumber were too heavy to transport any distance by road. Farmers brought their logs to a nearby sawmill and paid a few cents per board-foot to have them cut into lumber. Sawyers' account books reveal that some customers paid cash, but most others paid with farm produce, day labor on the mill owner's farm, or even work at the mill itself. Sawing usually began in earnest in the winter, when streams were running high, farming chores were slack, and the snowy roads made for easier sledding of logs and lumber. According to the diary kept by David Wight, Jr., he or one of his sons could usually be found working in the sawmill six days a week in December and January. Sawing continued into the spring as long as water levels were high, but by April, Wight and his sons often had to run their mill at night and work in their fields during the day. Sawing shifted to a more sporadic schedule as water levels dropped later in the spring, and the mill was generally shut down completely by the time haying season arrived in July. Although the museum demonstrates sawing throughout the year, most nineteenth-century sawmills were idle during the summer and early fall.

Gristmill

Corn to be ground drops into the hopper of one of the Gristmill's two pairs of millstones. The lower, or "bed" stone of the other pair is visible, along with the tools for "dressing" it

Unlike sawmills, which thrived during the winter, a gristmill was sometimes difficult to operate during the cold months. Ice and snow could build up rapidly around the exposed troughs, or buckets, of their slow-moving "gravity" waterwheels and lock up the mechanism for much of the season. Large "breast wheels," like the one reconstructed at the Village's Gristmill, were used extensively in New England during the late eighteenth and early nineteenth centuries. Since they were designed to take on water at about the height of their axles, or at breast height, they could be sited without building the high dams or long raceways often required by other designs. Needing only a low, gated

penstock and a close-fitting wooden "apron" to direct flowing water into the buckets, breast wheels could often be constructed and maintained relatively cheaply. Because they could also be designed with very wide buckets to make them more powerful, these wheels were often used to drive the machinery of early-nineteenth-century textile factories as well as the stones of gristmills.

Breast wheels undoubtedly powered the majority of New England's gristmills, probably including the three operating in the town of Sturbridge in 1833. The twin mill-stones in any of those mills would have taken only fifteen minutes or so to grind enough flour or meal to supply a family for a month. Since it would have required a farm wife an hour or two a day all month long to pound out such an amount in a mortar and pestle, gristmills had been regarded as necessary community services since medieval times. Almost every New England town sought to attract at least one miller among its earliest settlers and, as farmers could seldom haul a load of grain farther than five or six miles and still get back before nightfall, communities tried thereafter to ensure that an adequate number of mills were available. As late as the 1830s, they were still offering inducements to men who would build gristmills.

The Gristmill at the Village was built by combining old timbers and new lumber near the site of an early-nineteenth-century gristmill that had stood beside David Wight's sawmill. Once again on this spot, as soon as ice has left the Millpond in the spring, a penstock gate can be opened wide and a great breast wheel will be slowly turned by the weight of falling water in its buckets. This creaking movement drives the connecting shafts and wooden gears in the Gristmill basement, transmitting the awesome power that spins the millstone, vibrating the whole building. The twin granite millstones and associated machinery in the mill came from the Porter gristmill, which still stands in Hebron, Connecticut. The basic design of such milling machinery is very old, dating back at least to the traditional technologies of medieval Europe. A three thousand–pound "runner stone" rotates just a slight distance above a matching, but stationary, "bed stone" seated in the floor. Incised into the face of each stone are grooved patterns, designed to cross like scissor blades as the upper stone revolves. From the narrow gate of a wooden hopper, constructed as part of a cover for the stones, grain pours down through a hole in the runner stone and accumulates between the two millstones. As the runner stone turns, the grain is sheared into flour or meal, whose fineness depends on how closely the stones are set together. The fresh "grist" pours out into the meal chest in the floor. From there, in the 1830s, it would have been scooped up into the customer's bag or barrel and loaded into his cart for the trip home.

Farmers brought their grain to the mill to be ground into flour and meal for baking and provender for livestock. The miller was allowed by law to charge a fee or toll of one-sixteenth part of whatever grain was brought to him as payment for milling the rest. Millers consumed some of the grain in their own households and farms and used the rest in neighborhood exchange. By the 1830s, some country millers were replacing the traditional tolls with cash fees. Others moved in a different direction, becoming retail merchants who sold grain, flour, and meal directly to the growing number of rural families who were no longer farming.

Carding Mill

The great changes of the times, however, are nowhere in greater evidence than at the Carding Mill, the third mill on the Millpond. Small, independent wool carding establishments flourished in the countryside for a few decades even while the disparate processes of textile production were being completely mechanized in larger factories. In many a small mill neighborhood, they represented the first hint of the industrial future. Carding "engines," or machines that could replace the incredibly tedious work of preparing wool or cotton for spinning, had been developed during the British Industrial Revolution of the late eighteenth century. The British government tried to protect this technological achievement by prohibiting both the export of machinery designs and the

The roller card and batt card at the Carding Mill, two of the oldest operating pieces of textile machinery in the United States

emigration of artisans with technical knowledge, but skilled mechanics who had memorized plans for machinery slipped out of the country anyway. Despite the attempted embargo on knowledge, American-built carding machines began to appear as early as the 1780s. Since carding engines were small and required relatively little waterpower, by 1800 a rural entrepreneur could purchase machines from a manufacturer—either a British emigrant or a quick-to-learn New Englander—and develop a mill site with a modest capital investment.

In 1811, the Treasury Department estimated that almost every New England town had at least one carding mill. That same year, young Amasa Walker of Brookfield, Massachusetts, was sent on horseback to Slayton's carding mill with a large bundle of wool, which his mother intended to make into a coat for him. The new carding machine was "regarded as a wonderful invention," he later recalled, but "Mr. Slayton . . . was overrun with business; everybody wanted their wool carded, and his machine operated slowly." Mr. Slayton must have been very busy, indeed, since even the slowest of carding machines could do in a few minutes what had previously taken a whole day to do by hand. After washing, or "scouring," wool and picking out burrs at home, it still took many hours to prepare it for spinning. The wool fibers had to be disentangled, smoothed out, and shaped into cylindrical rolls for spinning by combing them in small batches between two "hand cards" fitted with hundreds of small wire teeth. Farm women were happy to shed such a time-consuming chore, and quickly became eager customers of the wonderful new mills. After 1811, the number of mills slowly declined as homespun cloth was replaced by factory-made textiles. Still, a significant number survived up through 1840 and beyond, turning a modest profit from the amount of home spinning still being done.

Oliver Hapgood's carding mill had survived in its original location in South Waterford, Maine, with its rare original machinery intact, until it was moved and restored at Old Sturbridge Village. The three waterpowered machines, dating from the 1820s, have been carefully maintained to demonstrate how the technology of the early Industrial Revolution was once used to make farm life a little easier. The heavy frames,

In the basement of the Carding Mill, iron gears, wooden pulleys, and leather belts transmit power from the enclosed tub wheel to the machinery above

drums, and pulleys of the machines are made of wood and appear simple enough to have been made by a country carpenter. However, the gears, shafts, and bearings of these ingenious "engines" are metal castings or forgings, built for durability and precision.

The wooden cover of the picker conceals a spike-toothed drum, turning at high speed, that loosens, fluffs, and cleans debris out of the scoured wool. Then it can be taken up on either carding machine, the "batt card" or the "roll card." Both these "marvelous inventions" comb out and straighten the tangled fibers of the wool by passing it back and forth between a succession of rotating drums or cylinders covered with "card clothing." This "clothing," much like the covering on paddle-shaped hand cards, is a leather backing fitted with thousands of closely spaced wire teeth. The carded fibers are drawn along on a large central drum, passing around and between numerous pairs of oppositely revolving cylinders. On the batt card, the wool leaving the machine is wound around a final drum in long gauzy layers to build up batts thick enough for stuffing or quilting. The roll card works differently. Its final cylinder takes up the wool and separates it into long, four-inch wide strips. They are then pulled off by a reciprocating "doffing comb" and rolled onto a fluted wooden cylinder to provide long fluffy rolls, or "rovings," ready for spinning. The batts and rolls produced in carding mills were much more uniform than any made by hand carding, and the service cost only a few cents per pound.

The carding machines are powered by a "tub wheel" mounted on a vertical shaft in the open basement of the mill. Vertical waterwheels have as long a history as horizontal ones, but the wood-encased tub wheel, spinning rapidly on its upright shaft, was a significant innovation when it was developed by rural millwrights in the 1820s. A powerful jet of water is directed by the sloping wooden penstock against the wheel's twenty-four cast-iron vanes. The wheel spins a sizable vertical shaft, and its cast-iron bevel gears drive two horizontal shafts, turning the large pulleys and heavy leather belts that power the machinery on the floor above. The roll card and batt card machines turn at the same speed as the tub wheel, but the picker rotates five or six times faster. The arrangements required for different speeds, involving larger and smaller pulleys, can be seen in the basement. On the floor above, each machine has two pulleys side by side: a "fast" pulley that engages the power and a "loose" pulley for idling. Simply by shifting a drive belt from "fast" to "loose," the mill operator can disengage any of his machines from the spinning gears and roaring water of the tub wheel.

Small carding mills, serving rural neighborhood markets, remained in operation into the middle of the nineteenth century. But they hinted at change of much greater scope. By the 1830s, carding machines were most commonly used in combination with machinery for spinning and weaving in New England's fast-growing woolen and cotton factories. On hundreds of medium-sized streams, small factories and manufacturing villages emerged throughout the New England countryside whose total production rivaled that of the huge enterprises at places like Lowell, Massachusetts, and Manchester, New Hampshire. There were three textile mills in Sturbridge, employing 244 people and producing nearly a million yards of cotton cloth in 1838. As manufactured textiles became ever cheaper, the production of cloth at home steadily dwindled, and New England's country carding mills gradually fell silent. With the rare and fortunate exception of the Hapgood Mill, they disappeared long ago.

CHAPTER FIVE

Artisans and Industry

THERE WAS, AS SAMUEL Goodrich remembered, "a great multiplying and diversifying of the occupations of society" during the early nineteenth century. For virtually everyone, how work was performed, how it was perceived, and often where it was done were changing in ways large and small. In New England, traditional ways of rural exchange, household production, and versatility were challenged by the cash economy, production for large-scale markets, and the increasing division of labor. The impact of this transformation was most dramatic in the cities, but it touched every rural community.

Opposite: Cluttered with tools, containers, and parts, and redolent of wood shavings, the Cooper Shop interior typifies an early-nineteenth-century craftsman's work space

Above: Apprenticeship was learning by doing, often with seemingly endless repetitions. It was the only path to mastery of a craft

The Traditions of Country Artisans

By today's standards, a working life in rural New England at the beginning of the nineteenth century was one of strenuous and exacting effort. Not only did farmers, sawyers, and millers make a living with their hands, but so did blacksmiths, cabinetmakers, coopers, potters, printers, tinners, shoemakers, wagonmakers, and tanners. By and large, goods were produced by practiced handwork, without mechanization or standardization. Artisans, or "mechanics" as they were usually called, worked from memory, without the use of elaborate plans or specifications and often without measurements. Their technique was shaped by the heft and feel of tools and materials, and craftsmen refined their skills over a lifetime of repetitive motions. Working in this fashion, some produced beautifully proportioned and finely crafted objects of enduring quality. Some trades—such as blacksmithing, housewrighting, stonemasonry, iron founding, and presswork in the printing office—tested strength and endurance. Less overtly strenuous trades, like shoemaking and tin work, demanded the monotonous execution of intricate tasks—often in the cold or in dim light.

New England craftsmen retained the terminology of English tradition, as "masters" trained young "apprentices" and hired "journeymen" to work in their shops. Yet entry into the trades was basically unrestricted and standards of practice went largely unregulated, except by customer preference and artisanal pride. Artisans, like virtually everyone else, learned their trades as youths by observing, imitating, and repeating the work of skilled adults. The most highly skilled trades had the longest apprenticeships, sometimes with formally binding "indentures" arranged between a youngster's father and the master. For many rural artisans the apprenticeship was far less formal, the agreement being merely an oral commitment and the length of time considerably less than the proverbial seven years. In small country shops, where trades were often practiced only part-time in conjunction with farming, craft skills were most often simply passed on to sons, nephews, and younger brothers.

The work life of all artisans alternated between times of intense productive effort and periods when the pace slackened or tasks were delayed in favor of farm chores. The tradesman, like the farmer and the miller, worked to the rhythm of the seasons and the measure of demand far more than to the regimen of the clock. Traditionally, master craftsmen took their journeymen and apprentices into their homes. Journeymen—trained artisans employed by the day—were usually young, unmarried, and in need of a place to live. As living alone was simply not an alternative, journeymen often lodged in their masters' households; apprentices, whether formally or casually bound, were customarily expected to do so. Besides being taught the "art and mystery" of the trade, these dependents were fed and clothed, usually taken to meeting, and sent to school. Many apprentices entered into their masters' families as if they were sons, but there were also instances of mistreatment followed by running away, and even pursuit. Occasionally, a young man would simply abandon the trade for some other venture once his apprenticeship was over; a few would try several apprenticeships in succession before settling on an occupation.

Many New England country craftsmen practiced two or even three trades; before 1820, most were also farmers. They exhibited an astonishing variety of skills in the process of working their farms and maintaining a "comfortable subsistence" or "competence" for their families. Early rural artisans produced goods to order as part of the local economic web of their communities. They were versatile producers in an economy of small markets and limited demand.

Opposite: The Cooper Shop, located on the road leading past the Freeman Farm

Cooper Shop

With curved and tapered wooden staves held tightly together by hoops of iron or bent sapling, coopered containers were once universally in use for storing goods in bulk and holding liquids of every kind. Coopers turned out impressive quantities of "dry" and "wet," or watertight, barrels, pails, and tubs, using only hand tools and virtually no measuring implements. In the countryside, coopers combined their trade with other kinds of woodworking as well as farming, exchanging staved containers for work and produce with customers living nearby.

The Cooper Shop at Old Sturbridge Village was originally owned by artisan Simeon Nash of Waldoboro, Maine, where he farmed in the warmer months and found winter employment making casks for shipping locally produced limestone. It is a single-story shop, two bays wide and a single bay deep, with a fireplace and chimney built into one corner. Many of its hand-hewn framing timbers appear to have been salvaged from an earlier structure. Small windows cast pale streams of light into the shadowy jumble of barrels, buckets, pails, half-finished tubs, bundles of stave stock, and piles of shavings that surround the coopers at their work.

The coopers use axes and froes (cutting blades mounted at right angles to the han-

dle) to cut and split the stock. Each straight piece of seasoned wood is locked into place on a shaving horse and given its curve and taper with a drawknife. The staves for each container must be shaped to fit precisely in three dimensions, so their edges are passed repeatedly across a jointer plane. Once the staves are carved, they are "raised up" together with a temporary working hoop and "headed," or closed up securely at one end. A second hoop driven onto the container locks the half-splayed staves together so they can be bent to close at the other end. The bending requires heat, produced by burning wood shavings in an iron basket, or "cresset," inside the barrel. As the heat relaxes wood fibers on the barrel's inner side, several heavy hoops—in progressively smaller diameters—are rapidly hammered on to bring the staves together. Once closed, the container is trussed with permanent hooping and heated again in a second firing to "set" the staves in a lasting bend.

Although Village coopers demonstrate the skills of their trade throughout the year, surviving account books of nineteenth-century country coopers tell a story of seasonal labor. During January, February, and early March a cooper would spend much of his time in the woods selecting saplings for hoop poles, choosing and cutting timber for next year's stave stock, hand-splitting it, and stacking it near his shop to dry. White oak was used to make wet barrels that could hold cider or pickling vinegar. Tight, dry containers such as butter firkins or meat barrels usually required white oak as well, although white ash and chestnut could be used. "Slack" barrels for storing apples, grain, or flour were fashioned from red oak; most household and dairy containers, including piggins—

Some of the tools of the cooper's trade: a jointer plane (top) and drawknife (bottom) used to shape and fit the staves and heads of barrels; a "croze" (farthest left) and a "howell" used to fit heads into the barrels

small pails with one stave left long to serve as a handle—larger buckets, and tubs of all
sizes were made of white pine or cedar.

From late March through May, country coopers turned their attention to farmwork; but as cows freshened and dairying began again in earnest, customers ordered new
containers or came for urgently needed repairs to those that had shrunk or been damaged
over the winter. Throughout the summer months coopers labored intensively in their
own fields. Beginning in late August, and continuing through September and early
October, they were busy making barrels for apples, grain, flour, and potatoes. In October
and November came orders for cider barrels at apple harvest and pressing time, and in
December, the beginning of the slaughtering season, for meat barrels.

A few rural coopers worked on a more commercial basis, making powder kegs
for a gunpowder works or, like Nash, producing limestone casks for a quarry. Most did
custom or "bespoke" work for their neighbors in exchange for goods or labor, rarely selling their wares for cash. But even for traditional craftsmen deep in the countryside, by
the 1830s there were glimmers of radical change on the horizon. New water-powered
pail factories were being built to mass-produce simple containers. They employed young
men at "setwork," for which they needed to know far less about their trade than traditional coopers.

The Pottery, or "pot shop" as Hervey Brooks called it

Pottery

New England's redware pottery tradition came from seventeenth-century England to the New World, where it flourished into the early nineteenth century. Then it slowly faded away, replaced by newer technologies. But one redware potter, Hervey Brooks of Goshen, Connecticut, about sixty miles southwest of Sturbridge, eluded historical oblivion. His "pot shop," surviving examples of shop equipment, his pottery, and his account books have been preserved at Old Sturbridge Village. Archaeological work at Brooks's original shop site, extensive analysis of his accounts, and careful reconstruction of local records have yielded a wealth of information about his work and life.

Hervey Brooks came to Goshen as a sixteen-year-old apprentice to farmer and potter Jesse Wadhams. He worked for about six years to learn the ancient craft and then started to make wares on his own in 1802. He began keeping daily accounts of his work during that year and married Polly Taylor of nearby Granville the following April. For nearly ten years young Brooks hired out his services to other potters, filling orders that demonstrated his mastery of more than two dozen different varieties and sizes of jugs, pitchers, pots, mugs, bowls, and platters. In 1814, he bought a house and land in a country neighborhood in Goshen called "South End," where he started farming and began to build his own pot shop and bottle-shaped brick pottery kiln.

Between 1818 and 1820, first in partnership with another potter and then working on his own, Brooks made and fired a great quantity of what he called "ware"—eighteen or nineteen kiln loads. Besides turning out thousands of milk pans, chamber pots, drinking vessels, and cooking pots at his wheel during those years, he had to rebuild the kiln in 1820 before firing the last two loads. When not at the shop, he was often busy digging and hauling clay and carting his wares to western Connecticut and New York State. Brooks tried to interest one of his sons in the trade, but Isaac Brooks ran away to Georgia in 1823, leaving a debt to his father both for the abandoned apprenticeship and the wagon he took for the trip!

After 1820, Brooks's potting work apparently slacked off and he did not record another firing for seven years. Then, from 1828 on, he regularly made and fired at least one kiln load of ware each year, always between June and November. On September 23, 1864, still keeping the accounts he had started in 1802, Hervey Brooks recorded the firing of his last load of pottery. On the same ledger page as the account of his wife's funeral, the eighty-five-year-old farmer and artisan recorded that he "made a kiln of ware this summer, consisting of Milkpans, some Pots, Pudding pans & Wash bowls, but mostly of Stove tubs and Flowerpots, and have this day finished burning the same."

Redware clay is gray in its original state, but turns brick-red when fired. It is found at many places in New England. Hervey Brooks carted his clay supplies to the pot shop from several open pits or "clay mines" on land he owned out behind his house. At the Hervey Brooks Pottery today, redware clay is piled up outside the shop and exposed to the weather for a time before being shoveled into the tub of the pug mill, where it is allowed to soak in water for several days. After the clay is ground and smoothed in the horse-powered mill, it is taken into the shop for drying and storage in a clay cellar.

Using a carefully reproduced potter's kick wheel, the potter shapes a lump of clay and, as if by magic, steadily and smoothly pulls the newly formed sides of a spinning pot up between his thumbs and fingers. "When the vessel is finished," according to an 1807 *Book of Trades*, "the workman cuts it off from the remaining part of the clay, and sets it aside to dry." Hundreds of pieces of "green" ware—actually a dusky gray—are set out to dry on the shelves that line the walls of the shop. In the profusion of repeated shapes are milk pans, cooking pots, drinking mugs, pitchers, and jugs of all sizes. Once dried, most of the pots are dipped into a liquid glaze that will give them a glossy, impermeable surface after firing. Like other early potters, Brooks used lead-based glazes, grinding the materials with water in a hand-powered glaze mill in his shop. Ingestion of lead could cause serious illness, and it was not unknown for potters to become sick from their work with glazes—something Brooks seems to have avoided.

Just across the road, the tall red-brick bottle kiln can hold five hundred pots or more, when they are carefully stacked and separated by bits of previously fired "kiln fur-

Above: Using his hands as a tool, a potter forms the neck and rim of a redware pitcher

Right: The legacy of Hervey Brooks: early-nineteenth-century redware vessels bearing his own maker's stamp

Sparks fill the Blacksmith Shop as two smiths alternate strikes at the anvil

niture." The kiln is a reconstruction based on archaeological excavations of kiln sites, frag-mentary images and descriptions, information about early-nineteenth-century building techniques, and the accumulated experience of Old Sturbridge Village potters. It is "burned" two or three times each year. Once the ware is loaded, the loading entrance is bricked up and sealed. Then fires are built in the "fire mouths" at either side of the base and are continuously fed for the next thirty-six hours or so. As the potters work in shifts to tend the fires, the kiln consumes at least two cords of wood, first hardwood and then pine, to reach a temperature of almost two thousand degrees Fahrenheit. After a gradual cooling that takes another full day, the doors are opened for "drawing the kiln" or unloading the finished wares for use and sale.

As in other neighborhoods, little cash changed hands in the economic networks around Goshen. Hervey Brooks occasionally exchanged a "lot of wares" for a clock from the Sanfords, clockmakers who lived down the road, and in turn traded that for other goods and services. He often exchanged farm labor and products with Isaac Wadhams, who once bought three thousand bricks. Wadhams used those bricks to build a smokehouse, which, coincidentally, was later moved to the museum and is now preserved at the Freeman Farm. Brooks sometimes sold his wares in "wholesale" lots to stores and dealers, but more frequently he traded pottery a few pieces at a time with neighbors and townspeople for produce and labor.

Brooks's long years of detailed accounts show that he combined pottery with an amazing range of other activities. He did his own farmwork, traded butter and cheese, hired out his horse and wagon, and labored for his neighbors—picking apples, haying, hoeing potatoes, grafting apple trees, carting grain to a mill, and butchering. He taught a singing school in his neighborhood and occasionally undertook carpentry and blacksmithing. It is also clear from his records that he sometimes kept a small store, selling salt, tobacco, tea, and rum.

By the middle of the nineteenth century the demand for redware pottery had withered away under the pressure of competition from imported English ceramics and American tinware. The population of "South End" declined over the years, and Hervey Brooks sold fewer and fewer milk pans and pitchers. By turning out stovepipes, drain tiles, and flowerpots, he kept his pottery business alive long after it had gone out of style.

Blacksmith Shop

The ringing peal of hammer and anvil echoes through the neighborhood around the millpond. The sharp odors of coal smoke and hot iron permeate the darkness of the stone shop, where metals heated yellow-hot are hammered into shape before they cool and every forging of a weld sends up a shower of flying sparks. A myriad of specialized hammers, chisels, punches, and less familiar tools like hardies, fullers, flatters, and swages fill the shop's racks and line benches and shelves. Dozens of tongs with differently shaped jaws hang close at hand before the forge, ready to grip the fiery shape of any work. As Village blacksmiths heat and reshape iron and steel, making and repairing a great miscellany of tools and hardware, they are demonstrating the traditional skills of a trade once vital to every rural community.

By the 1830s, blacksmiths in rural New England were undertaking several different kinds of work. Some, usually located in manufacturing neighborhoods or growing center villages, became specialized producers of edge tools, nails, or machinery and parts. They often worked in shops with three or more men and sent their products to ware-

houses and dealers for distribution. Along the busiest roads were blacksmiths who worked only as wheelwrights or limited their work to shoeing horses. Other smiths plied their trade for wages, working at carriage-making shops or repairing machinery in the textile mills.

The Blacksmith Shop

Many blacksmiths, especially out in the countryside, took work of almost every kind, shoeing horses and oxen, fashioning the countless small items needed in the community, and repairing anything from pins to plowshares. Although commercially manufactured tools and hardware had become widely available, they broke or wore out and needed mending. Country blacksmiths worked mostly on farm tools and household utensils but also did work for sawyers and neighborhood craftsmen.

Iron and steel, the "black metals," were the blacksmith's principal materials. New metal stock came from New England furnaces, or from Sweden and Russia, and could be purchased in a wide variety of sizes and shapes from city warehouses and most country merchants. Old iron could be reused, and many rural smiths took it in exchange for their work. The most widely used fuel for the forge was charcoal, still readily available in the countryside where charcoal kilns used the wood from land clearing. However, some New England blacksmiths were using soft coal from England as early as 1825, and its use was increasing in areas close to major shipping routes by the 1830s.

Moses Wilder's blacksmith shop, now at Old Sturbridge Village, was probably built shortly after 1802, when he purchased land adjacent to a quarry operated by his wife's uncles and cousins in the outlying country neighborhood of Bolton, Massachusetts, about thirty miles northeast of Sturbridge. Wilder's solid, granite-walled shop was undoubtedly built with stone and labor from the quarry. There are no surviving records of Wilder's blacksmithing enterprise, but the daily operations of his shop, and many similar ones, can be construed from a diversity of written and material records of country smiths. In particular, the account books of Emerson Bixby, studied in tandem with the archaeology of his shop site in Barre, Massachusetts, create a compelling picture of a rural ironworker's tasks.

Blacksmithing work picked up in the early spring, when preparations for plowing brought in plowshares, harrows, ox chains, and the iron parts of yokes and harnesses

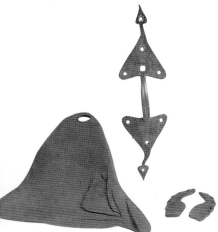

Above: Products of the country blacksmith's work: an iron plowshare with multiple repairs, an eye-catching door handle, and a two-piece shoe for an ox

Right: Used iron accumulates outside the Blacksmith Shop

to be readied for use. Horses and oxen then had to be reshod for summer work, and the frequency of repairs to carts, wagons, plows, and other damaged implements increased steadily from March through June. Like most able-bodied men in the countryside, a black-smith dropped the tools of his trade to join in the labor of haying through July and early August. By September, preparations for fall and winter work called for more shoeing and vehicle repair and brought a steady demand for parts and repairs from nearby sawyers, millers, and cider mill owners. The second peak in the blacksmith's cycle of work, often even exceeding the busy days of June, came in November and December. Readying farm-ers for their winter logging season, country blacksmiths were usually engaged in fitting horses and oxen with winter shoes, making and repairing axes, and working on sleighs and sleds. The flow of work declined sharply in January, however, and the pace did not pick up again until preparations for spring plowing resumed in March.

Opposite: Weaving strips of splint to make a basket

The blacksmith's trade was changing, not disappearing, in New England, and versatile country smiths were able to hang on in their neighborhoods through the mid-dle of the nineteenth century. Muscular young men continued to apprentice—it took years to learn metalworking—but less often than in the past. More of them went to city machine shops and fewer stayed in the countryside. Moses Wilder, it seems certain, taught the craft to his son Abraham, who carried it on in the Bolton shop. Emerson Bixby, who had no sons, apparently never took an apprentice, relying instead on days' work from his neighbors when he needed an extra pair of hands.

At Old Sturbridge Village, Wilder's shop now sits across the road from Bixby's house, and the trade they both practiced lives on in the skilled daily work of the museum's blacksmiths.

Basketmaking

Basketmaking in rural New England represented two distinctive traditions, English and Native American, which by the 1830s were considerably intertwined. Indispensable as baskets were, their production was a subsistence handcraft, not a path to wealth. Not only were they laborious to make, but by the 1830s European-made light baskets were available in country stores, and New England Shaker communities were beginning to produce them as well.

Wood splint, willow shoots, and straw were the materials New England's peo-ple used to make practical woven containers of great variety. Sturdy round or square bas-kets with high curved handles were used for carrying produce from the garden or goods to market. Lighter baskets, sometimes with matching covers, were used to store sewing materials and a miscellany of small household supplies. In fields and orchards, strongly made and sizable gathering baskets were loaded with apples, potatoes, and corn. Among the dozens of shapes and designs produced by rural basketmakers there were ox muzzles, cheese baskets, egg baskets, and even eel traps. Tall rectangular baskets held great heaps of unprocessed wool at the carding mill, and farmers winnowed their corn through bas-ketware sieves, called "riddles."

Basketmakers at the Village continue the handcraft tradition. They can usually be seen replicating the traditional English or "Yankee" designs of wood-splint basketry. But they reproduce a wide variety of basket styles from the museum's collections, at times copying Native American baskets, often decorated with stamped or hand-painted designs, that had been made for trade. By the early nineteenth century, basketmaking in both cultures shared a number of materials and techniques, including the production of splint baskets in oak and ash. Oak must be split and shaved into splints, but the more malleable black ash logs can be pounded with wooden mauls until the wood separates into thin strips along its growth rings. This "splint" is then shaped into different widths and thicknesses with a knife and woven into a great variety of patterns and shapes, dictated by tradition and the basketmaker's eye for form. Splint is shaped wide and thick for heavy uses like gathering baskets, but for fine, closely woven baskets it must be light and narrow. Finally, rims and handles are attached, often bent from well-soaked strips of hickory. The entire process of the craft, from pounding the logs to weaving the splint and shaping handles, is accomplished with only a few simple hand tools—as well as a practiced hand and eye.

Trades Reshaped and Specialized

By the 1830s many traditional country artisans were starting to lose their favored position in local markets. Increasingly, they found themselves in competition with specialized manufacturers, large and small, who were producing less costly and sometimes superior products. Tinware, farm implements, tools, and furniture were being mass-produced in city and village shops, undercutting rural potters, blacksmiths, and cabinetmakers. Country stores, guided by commerce and consumer demand, began to compete directly with local artisans by stocking articles produced by new manufacturers. The farmer-craftsmen who had made versatility a virtue had not disappeared by the 1830s, but they were much fewer. In their place appeared a different system of production, in which many shops now specialized in the manufacture of large numbers of items for the market in general, not for specific customers. In some trades, enterprising manufacturers hired semiskilled craft workers to make parts or assemble components. Over the better roads and transportation links of the 1830s, goods were distributed very widely, sold to stores or peddlers for resale, and shipped in larger wholesale lots to distant markets.

These transformations in production were slowly leading to changes in the way craftsmen experienced and perceived their work. Traditionally, artisans' work had been thoroughly intertwined with family life, but by the 1830s work was more often performed away from home in the wider public world. Workers and procedures alike became more specialized, and cash wages and cash prices were beginning to overtake the customary exchanges of goods and labor. Standardized products and mechanized techniques became more common, and regular hours started to replace the variable habits and seasonal cycles of traditional tradesmen. Some rural craftsmen, such as blacksmiths, were

Opposite: Shoemakers "stick to their lasts," bottoming brogans in the Shoe Shop. In the 1830s they would have worked twelve to fourteen hours a day

spending more and more time repairing tools and hardware, and doing much less original fabrication. Tinworkers were steadily gaining markets and expanding their numbers, while redware potters were gradually losing theirs. And shoemakers, even in their small shops, were involved in standardized production for a mass market. Increasingly, work was being performed for the market, as the traditional values of "getting by" were gradually supplanted by new ambitions to "get ahead."

Shoe Shop

Very cold overnight temperatures will almost always harden the sewing wax and freeze the water in the small tub at the Shoe Shop. Starting a fire in the tiny cast-iron stove is usually the first chore of the day for shoemakers at the Village, since leathers to be worked must soak in water and soft wax is needed to coat the thread. Once this small building heats up on a winter morning, warming fingers can go to work stitching or pegging soles in the light of nine large windows, closely spaced around the walls. Smooth pieces of clean-smelling leather have been cut to patterned sizes for soles, and piles of fin-

ished uppers await soaking and then stretching on the lasts. Traditional low-seated shoe-maker's benches, and an innovative "stand-up" bench, collect a profusion of awls, knives, punches, bristles, waxes, threads, needles, and wooden pegs. Wooden lasts, clamps and straps, pegging jacks, and cutting boards hang on nails or lean conveniently against the walls, and a clutter of leather scraps, wood chips, and ashes tends to pile up near the stove.

Such workrooms seem little different from the traditional custom shops where shoes were made to order and repaired for the populace of nearby communities. However, by the 1830s these small shops were, by the thousands, producing "sale" shoes for the wholesale trade. Managed by manufacturers and storekeepers, this trade was shipping shoes to markets far and wide. In Massachusetts, more people were employed in shoe-making than in any occupation besides farming. Some twenty-three thousand men and fifteen thousand women, mostly rural, were working at the shoe and boot trade in 1837, producing 15 million pairs of shoes and 1.5 million pairs of boots. In Worcester County alone, 7 percent of the total population worked at stitching and pegging nearly 3 million pairs of shoes. Shoemaking took place in small country shops and homes and depended almost completely upon handwork; but it was still an industry of mass production, open-ing the way for the mechanized factories that appeared later in the century. This emerging system did not completely eliminate the custom shoemakers, but it drastically rearranged the old certainties and hierarchies of the trade.

Women and girls usually worked at sewing together the shoe "uppers" in their homes, while men did the heavier work of "bottoming," attaching the soles and heels. The men sometimes worked at home, but more often in small, "ten-footer" shoe shops that became common features of the rural landscape. For the most part, it was a young man's—and young woman's—trade, calling upon skills that could be acquired relatively quickly, in a matter of months. Available records indicate that most shoemakers were under the age of thirty, and virtually all under forty. Many a son of a struggling farmer took to stitching and pegging shoes. Shoemakers were paid a cash wage, outside the web of the rural economy, and a steady worker bottoming shoes could average seventy-five cents a day, comfortably more than farm labor paid. In many communities, the trade was so attractive to young men that larger-scale farmers were becoming worried about a short-age of help.

The putting-out system for manufacturing shoes for the market was developed in eastern Massachusetts during the late eighteenth century and then spread more widely through New England in the early nineteenth. Entrepreneurs working out of "central shops," and sometimes storekeepers, purchased leather and other raw materials, oversaw the cutting out of parts in various patterns and sizes, and sent them out to homes and shops to be assembled. Young women, usually daughters of farmers and artisans, were hired to "close" and "bind," or sew and line, the soft leather upper parts of shoes for three to five cents a pair. The work was collected and then parceled out to the men, who drew the uppers over wooden lasts and stitched or pegged them to the sole leathers. Driving wooden pegs through sole and upper parts was the faster and cheaper method, and it became widely used after a machine for producing great quantities of the thin, pointed pegs was developed.

After the shoes were bottomed, they were returned to the central shop, packed in old barrels or wooden shoe cases, and shipped out on freight wagons to agents and dealers in the cities. Durable cowhide shoes and thick-soled boots were the usual products of the country shops. These standardized items, made on "straight" lasts rather than lefts and rights, constituted a revolution in available footwear for ordinary people. They were commonly available in New England's general stores, but greater quantities were shipped out of Boston, Providence, and New York to every location in the United States, as well as to Mexico, the Caribbean, and South America. Some merchant-manufacturers specialized in "slave brogans," shoes sent directly to plantations in the South and the West Indies.

Broom Making

In the early nineteenth century, broom making became a significant rural industry in New England, supplying a humble utensil that was in demand by city and country households increasingly concerned with cleanliness. Brooms were produced in scattered locations throughout the region, but the industry was concentrated in the Connecticut River valley of Massachusetts. Here broomcorn, the sorghum-like crop whose fibrous stalks made the most functional and longest-lasting brooms, was widely cultivated. The brooms were fashioned on simple hand-operated machines in small shops or larger "factories" that sometimes employed eight or ten workers. By the mid-1830s, more than a million brooms were being produced for shipment to wholesale merchants in Hartford and New York City.

Producing round brooms in the style, and with the technology, of the 1830s

The machines used in the museum's demonstration of broom making are reproductions of early-nineteenth-century originals. Simple enough to have been constructed by a local woodworker, the machines hold the twine or wire that binds a broom together under tension, so that the worker can keep the broom handle turning steadily while wrapping it tightly with strands of bushy broomcorn. The skill is not difficult to learn, and a good broom maker today, as in the 1830s, can produce a finished broom in less than half an hour. The distinctive round, woven broom design used at the Village represents one of several varieties commonly produced for the early-nineteenth-century market, including whisks, short hearth brooms, and the long-handled, wire-bound flat brooms that are more familiar today.

Tin Shop

According to an 1837 version of *The Book of Trades*, tinners "require cleverness, but not much real skill." No doubt New England's tin workers worried very little about such opinions, since their business was expanding dramatically during the early nineteenth century. Like shoemakers, tinners were full-time artisans who produced for markets far

The Tin Shop in the Center Village. A tinner lounges briefly outside before returning to work

A tinner or "tinman," wearing the paper hat often favored by artisans in his trade, shapes tinplate on his swedge

beyond their localities. They sold tinware at retail from their own shops and supplied goods wholesale to country stores and sometimes to large city warehouses or dealers shipping to the West or South. Most also used peddlers to distribute their goods in less populated parts. The largest shops sent their own employees out in wagons loaded with assortments of shiny tinware. Tinners preferred cash, but accepted the ways of rural exchange and took many kinds of goods in trade: rags, scrap brass and copper, feathers, and even cow horns. These goods were stockpiled until quantities were sufficient for resale to paper mills, foundries, and makers of mattresses or combs.

Tin shops could be large establishments employing journeymen and apprentice tinners as well as "japanners," decorators, and peddlers, but there were also many small shops run by one or two men. At Old Sturbridge Village, a small shop building of the kind that tinners often owned or rented sits on the far corner of the Parsonage lot, opposite the Tavern. This refurbished structure, which was originally part of an early-nineteenth-century house and workshop complex in the town of Sturbridge, depicts one of the thousands of small artisans' shops, now disappeared, that were once concentrated in New England's center villages.

The tinner, or sometimes "tinman," works with thin iron sheets coated with pure tin, and wire for stiffening seams. In the 1830s, tinplate was imported from England, usually through a Boston merchant. It arrived in elmwood boxes, each containing 225 ten-by-fourteen-inch sheets. If the materials could not be picked up by the tinner himself, they could be ordered by letter and shipped out by teamster. The solder that seals the seams of early tinware never appears in records of supplies purchased because tinners made their own, combining tin and molten lead.

The Tin Shop's equipment is a combination of traditional hand tools and early-nineteenth-century innovation. A small, charcoal-burning firepot to heat the soldering "coppers" would have been made right in the shop. Hand tools, including an assortment of anvil-like "stakes," plus shears, hammers, coppers, "swedges," chisels, pliers, and punches, had traditionally been all a tinman needed, but new machinery was changing the face of the trade. New England machinists tackled the problem of mechanizing and speeding up the manufacturing process, and in 1804 Eli Parsons and Calvin Whiting of Dedham, Massachusetts, patented small hand-cranked machines for "burring," "wiring," and "setting down." Over the next decades, these devices, along with other machines for "grooving" and "folding," were widely adopted. A working set of tin machines has been painstakingly reproduced for use in the Village's Tin Shop today, so that the tin-man's "cleverness" can be seen in full production.

Undramatic as these machines may seem, they could fold tinplate, turn edges, and roll wire into creases with such speed and precision that tinware prices dropped markedly while production increased severalfold. The time served in apprenticeships grew shorter. Young boys could commonly expect to finish their apprenticeships in about three or four years and then earn up to a dollar a day in credits or goods as a working journeyman. Every item produced was made from a pattern, sometimes designed on the spot but usually taken from the shop's standing collection. Consumers proved eager for household utensils such as colanders, pails, washbowls and washbasins, round pans, dippers, measures, and cannisters. Tinners also produced milk pans, "nests" of dry and liquid measures, oil lamps, lanterns, foot stoves, tea- and coffeepots, bakers, tin kitchens, sconces, and skimmers. Some shops produced decorated tinware, coating coffeepots, tea caddies, trays, and small trunks with dark "japan" varnish that ranged from golden brown to almost black. Women, probably working in their houses, were often employed to add stenciled or freehand painted designs.

The Tin Shop on the Common today portrays an enterprise that concentrates, as hundreds of small shops did, on the manufacture of plain tinware. Dozens upon dozens of bright household wares are stacked on its shelves—valued and fast-selling consumer goods of the 1830s. Starting from such small beginnings, a number of enterprising early-nineteenth-century tinmen expanded their businesses and found great prosperity. The "real skill" of their work, they found, was in shrewd business calculation.

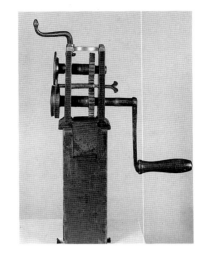

Tinsmiths used simple, hand-operated machines to expedite their work

Printing Office

At the beginning of the nineteenth century, rural printers could be found in about one in every five or six New England towns. They often did not publish newspapers, which flourished only in cities and county seats; instead they found "a more lucrative employment," as one of them said, by devoting "the whole of our attention to Book-work." Printing was a chancy business, requiring substantial investment in printing presses, at least two or three fonts of type with several thousand pieces each, and large quantities of paper stock. Many rural offices opened with great ambition, only to close after a few years.

The three-room building that portrays the Printing Office at Old Sturbridge Village is a structure once owned by Isaiah Thomas (1749–1831), the famed American printer who ensured his freedom to publish during the Revolution by moving his presses from Boston to the inland county seat of Worcester, about eighteen miles northeast of

The composing room at the Printing Office, with type cases, an ancient proof press in the far corner, and composing table

Overleaf: The Printing Office

Sturbridge. The building, dating from about 1780 and one of several used in Thomas's large operation, originally stood beside the Worcester County Courthouse. It has been substantially restored, based on early illustrations that record its original appearance, and is now used to depict the book and job printing, country bookstore, and bookbinding business of a country printer of the 1820s and 1830s. There are few surviving business records of rural New England printers of this period; a fortunate exception is the extensive papers of the Merriam family of Brookfield, Massachusetts, which Old Sturbridge Village has used in understanding the printer's life and work. The Merriams' story has a strong connection with the building as well, since senior partner Ebenezer Merriam had been Isaiah Thomas's last apprentice.

Printers were a distinctive sort of craftsman, whose work demanded both high literacy and mechanical aptitude, precision as well as strength. Tasks in the Village's Printing Office today include the hand-setting of lead type; meticulous correcting of proofs; and printing to paper, which requires a heavy pull on the hand-operated press for each impression. In the composing room, "quoins" and "shooting sticks" are used as wedges and tapping rods to lock type into frames, or "chases," for printing. On cold, dark winter afternoons, stiffening fingers and straining eyesight drive typesetters to move their trays back and forth between the stoves and the windows. (The Merriams' printing office inventory in 1824 listed eight candlesticks, nearly triple the number found in most households. They were used to illuminate the wearisome toil of ten people—often still working at eight o'clock at night.) The iron-framed Peter Smith press, a handsome example of the new nation's manufacturing expertise that was in wide use after 1825, has to be inked

before the printing of each sheet. The Village's printers count themselves fortunate that rollers, which are much easier to manipulate, began to replace old-fashioned leather ink balls in the 1830s.

Like most formally recognized trades, printing was considered men's work, but women were more likely to be found in printing offices than in most other shops. Very few women ever worked at the press, but printers' daughters and wives often learned to set type, and some even became recognized as expert compositors. Bookbinding was a craft allied to printing, very often carried on as part of the same business and under the same roof. Women were usually employed at folding "signatures" of printed sheets and stitching them together. Men then finished the work, "casing" books in bindings of stiffened paper covered with leather, cloth, or colorful marbled paper. Country printing offices might produce as many as twenty thousand volumes a year, and could employ from two people to eight or more, including journeymen, apprentices, and women as bookbinders.

The country printer's bookstore stocked copies of each of the books the office had produced, as well as many printed elsewhere, along with almanacs, blank books and forms, stationery, writing materials, slates and pencils for school, and often maps and engravings. The bookstore's best local customers were ministers, doctors, and lawyers who needed books in their work and who often paid in cash, but local artisans and farmers who supplied goods and services to the office also kept accounts there. Local printing jobs—including commercial forms, bills and labels, broadsides and notices,

A restored "acorn frame" press of the 1830s dominates the press room, where a freshly printed sheet is put up to dry on the rack

pamphlets commissioned by local voluntary societies, and ministers' sermons—brought in additional income. Bookstore sales and job printing were important in the community but were far overshadowed by the printer's specialized involvement in the regional and national book trade.

By the 1830s, country book printers in New England were part of an expanding network of book production and distribution that covered the Northeast and extended into the West and South. Through their ties to major centers of publishing in Boston, Philadelphia, and New York, printers took on "book-work" either as independent publishers or on contract for others. Contract printing involved shipping the printed books unbound to the publisher at a price set by previous negotiation. When printers published independently they marketed their books through a complicated series of exchanges with other publishers, large and small.

Rural printers worked actively to create a market for their assortments of books. They sold some in their own bookstores but delivered most to country storekeepers in surrounding towns, taking in return all manner of goods—flour, meat, fish, lumber, molasses, tea and coffee, lamp oil, cloth, and ribbons and laces. The goods were used to pay journeymen, to feed and clothe the printer's family and apprentices, and to balance accounts with creditors who were unwilling to accept books. Cash payments were rare and most of the business was built on credit, so the affairs of many country printers were complex and uncertain even while sustaining a fairly comfortable way of life.

The business of country printing depended on an expanding market for books. New Englanders had always been among the world's most literate people, but in the seventeenth and eighteenth centuries they owned few books by today's standards. In the early nineteenth century, New Englanders and other Americans were becoming increasingly avid consumers of printed matter. Bibles and other religious books had always been staples of American printing, along with works of law and medicine. Novels were popular among urban readers, but still distrusted in the countryside. The true "best sellers" were almanacs and schoolbooks. Spellers, arithmetics, readers, geographies, and history texts were far more widely available by the 1830s than they had been even two decades earlier. Beginning a national tradition of "self-help" literature, books of advice and instruction were an expanding market—from cookbooks and builder's guides to texts on health and motherhood.

To produce their books, printing offices required a greater capital investment than most crafts and hired larger workforces. More journeymen were employed in the printing business than in most other trades, and the old traditions of apprenticeship were slower to change. By the early nineteenth century, young men of fifteen or sixteen were starting apprenticeships bound by informal verbal agreements that required four or five years service, and they were still living in the master's household. Although they seldom received wages for their daily work, apprentices were sometimes paid for "overwork" they might wish to take on as they became more skillful.

Country printers had to be both craftsmen and capitalists, yet their economic networks could adapt only partially to the rapidly commercializing economy of the 1830s. Their customers were widely dispersed and cash was in very short supply. When urban publishers and paper suppliers began to demand cash payments instead of accepting books on exchange, rural printing began to decline. By mid-century there were hardly any "old-style" printer-publishers left in the countryside.

Clockmaking

Clocks were and are still among the most complex of handcrafted artifacts, requiring the skills not only of clockmakers themselves but of blacksmiths, brass workers, cabinet-makers, engravers, and painters. The story of clockmakers and their creations emerges in a different way at the Village, not in an artisan's shop but in the J. Cheney Wells Clock Gallery, which houses the museum's renowned collection of New England clocks. The high art, intricate technology, and everyday economics of early American clockmaking are presented here, where more than one hundred clocks and timepieces tick away year-round, many sounding on the hour. The Museum's holdings are based on the extraordinary personal collection of J. Cheney Wells, a founder of Old Sturbridge Village.

In the Clock Gallery, visitors can savor the strikingly or sometimes subtly different clocks that these craftsmen created collaboratively. Stately tall clocks with elegant cases and dials and finely made brass movements are displayed along with wooden-works shelf clocks mass-produced for wider markets. Tall clocks, both urbane and rustic, and numerous examples of mantel, wall, and shelf clocks present a remarkable variety of case designs, finishes and materials, decorative dials, and precision mechanisms. Visitors to the Gallery can compare the gilt and glitter of a delicate girandole clock by Lemuel Curtis to the massive iron-geared mechanism of a meetinghouse tower clock that turns hands on a dial set in the Gallery's outer wall.

Many of the collection's most significant clocks were made by members of New England's premier clockmaking family—Simon Willard, his brother Aaron, and their

Opposite, top: *Pillar and scroll shelf clock by Seth Thomas, c. 1825*

Opposite, bottom: *Tall clock by Simon Willard, 1801*

Right: *Girandole clock by Lemuel Curtis of Concord, Massachusetts, c. 1816*

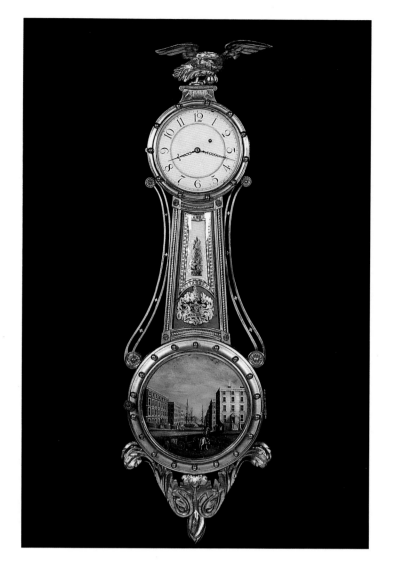

sons—or by some of their former apprentices. In the late eighteenth and early nineteenth centuries, the Willards set the standard for both quality and economic success and maintained a continuing tradition of technical innovation. The Gallery presents Willard and Willard-influenced tall clocks, as well as examples of distinctive Willard "patent timepieces," banjo-shaped and wall-mounted, that became highly popular symbols of refinement and prosperity. Along with the Willard lineage of clocks, however, the Gallery displays the work of other important makers and of less well known country clockmakers, versatile rural craftsmen who produced distinctive works of horological art while also trading goods and labor with their neighbors in the agricultural economy.

New England's finest tall clocks and patent timepieces remained elegant artifacts for the well-to-do. But, with its display of the inexpensive clocks of the 1830s that were being made for wider markets by Eli Terry, Seth Thomas, and other Connecticut craftsmen, the Gallery also documents dramatic economic and technological change. These entrepreneurs were "Americanizing" clockmaking by replacing brass movements with parts made of native woods—oak, cherry, and maple. They transformed clockmaking into a true mass-production industry and brought the measurement of time not only to the ordinary households of New England, but ultimately to eager consumers all across America.

CHAPTER SIX

The Common

THE CENTER VILLAGE, WITH ITS GRASSY COM-
mon, at least one meetinghouse, and a growing cluster of
dwellings and shops, was the heart of the early-nineteenth-century New England town. Many a sleepy town center was transformed into a thriving hub of social life and commercial activity
in the years after 1800. Merchants, craftsmen, tavernkeepers,
and professional men made their livings around the common,
providing goods and services to outlying neighborhoods as
improved roads, better conveyances, and increasing prosperity
brought farming families to the village center to trade, visit, and
worship. The new rush of economic activity brought wider
opportunities for domestic abundance and fresh visions of progress and social improvement.

Commons themselves, the central open spaces that most communities set aside
next to the first meetinghouse, changed as the center villages grew. The earliest commons
were generally neglected and treeless pieces of open land. After 1800, however, they
took on a neater, better-tended look. Many of the towns' most prosperous and influential
families began to live in the center villages, and more than any earlier generation of New
Englanders, they were concerned about the appearance of their homes, grounds, and
neighborhood. By the 1830s, village residents were imposing their genteel tastes on the
common, keeping the grass well mowed and planting shade trees.

Clustered around the common and along the roads that passed by it were the
white- or yellow-painted houses of respectable center village families, with their dooryards neatly fenced, piles of firewood meticulously stacked, and kitchen gardens carefully tended. The power of a newly unfolding prosperity was clearly visible in these
dwellings, expressed in new furnishings, new fashions, and contagious ideals of refine-

*Opposite: Fashionably dressed dwellers on
the Common are silhouetted against the
Greek Revival facade of the Center
Meetinghouse*

*Above: The sitting room chamber at the
Parsonage displays the artifacts of genteel cleanliness: looking glass and wash-
stand with basin, towel, ewer,
and—discreetly tucked under the bed—
chamber pot*

*Overleaf: The Center Village from the
Towne House garden*

ment. Although a well-to-do progressive farm or two might reach the edge of the common, most village houses, whether modest or grand, were sited with their barns and sheds on smallish lots with room enough only for gardens and a few livestock. At least one imposing meetinghouse (sometimes there were two or three) provided a focal point, and workshops and commercial structures were interspersed among the residences.

During the period of rapid village growth between 1790 and 1840, many center village houses, stores, workshops, taverns, and offices were built new, and most older structures were altered. Before the villages began to grow, housewrights in rural New England often built with less regard for symmetry than convenience. Practicality, much more than aesthetics, often determined the placement of windows and doors, and seemingly haphazard, though functional, changes or additions were common. Many houses had no entryways to protect family privacy and were entered directly from the road. Their siting on the landscape often followed the points of the compass—thus, they frequently turned their backs on the road or "stood half-cornerwise" against it. Traditional New England houses were built around a massive central chimney. Most were small, with two, three, or four rooms in a single-story or story-and-a-half plan. Others were built in the two-story lean-to (today's "saltbox") pattern with a steeply sloping back roof that provided additional space on the first floor.

The most up-to-date builders in eighteenth-century New England were producing substantial two-story houses first in the English Georgian style and then in the updated and simplified Federal style; these houses became the hallmark of gentility in country towns. In such dwellings, the main facade presented a dignified standard of symmetry, with a center doorway flanked by windows. Such houses almost always faced the road, with the entryway opening to a central hallway and staircase running between two separate chimneys. Visitors stepped into the hall before entering the family's living space, and rarely did one have to cross through one room to get to another. These amenities were at first only available to the well-to-do, but the design concepts were gradually accepted and adapted by builders and householders all across New England.

Architectural styles and fashions that were adopted rapidly in seaport cities came more slowly and partially to rural areas, where a jumbled overlapping of newer and more traditional house forms usually prevailed. Fairly early in the eighteenth century, Georgian conceptions of symmetry and privacy had begun to influence many of the dwellings built in the countryside. The great majority of eighteenth-century rural houses retained the central-chimney plan, but many—including the Parsonage, Fitch House, Freeman Farmhouse, and Fenno House at Old Sturbridge Village—have a small entryway. The Parsonage even has a symmetrical facade, but only the Salem Towne House has the central hallway and paired-chimney plan of the classic Federal (or earlier Georgian) style. Some country housewrights, even into the early years of the nineteenth century, continued building small vernacular houses according to local traditions. These dwellings, like the village's Bixby House, often display distinctive features characteristic of their neighborhoods. Renovations might only alter outward appearances, with, for example, the addition of a central doorway opening directly into the old uneven arrangements of living space.

Rural builders came to work in the new styles by copying and adapting exam-

ples they saw and by using the detailed practical examples available in illustrated architectural handbooks. Housewright's guides, like Asher Benjamin's *Country Builder's Assistant*, published in 1797 and in its fourth edition in 1805, carried the Federal look across the New England landscape. During the 1830s, the Greek Revival style, popular for public buildings and mansions in the cities for several decades, brought its characteristic temple-like columns and bold geometric trim to rural homes and meetinghouses, and turned the gable ends of houses to face the street. Another of Benjamin's books, *The Practical House Carpenter*, published in 1830, helped this new style gain rapid dominance as the most common design for houses built in New England's country towns.

Houses were becoming larger at the very time families were becoming smaller. Among all the dwellings in Shirley, Massachusetts, the number of two-story houses increased from less than a third in 1798 to more than half by 1832. Meanwhile, the greater number of rooms made for a clearer separation of household activities. "Back rooms" for storage became commonplace, rooms on the second floor provided more bedchambers and parents' beds were disappearing from parlors. Many traditional patterns remained, however. Most families still took their meals in the parlor or in the kitchen; only a few families had a separate dining room. Children and other household members—relatives, domestics, laborers, and apprentices alike—usually shared beds as well as space in garrets, hallways, and upstairs chambers, which were often unfinished.

Cleanliness, order, and improving notions of "neatness and tastefulness" were vigorously promoted in Lydia Maria Child's *The American Frugal Housewife* and in a host of other widely distributed publications brimming with domestic advice. As Emily Farrar, author of *The Young Lady's Friend*, noted in 1836, country folk were still obliged to "wash at the pump in the yard, or at the sink in the kitchen." This made real bathing impossible, and cleanliness for most New Englanders still ended at the neck, the arms, and the ankles. But by the 1830s, "chamber sets," matching basins and ewers for private bathing, were starting to appear in the bedchambers of center village homes. Even in the countryside, traditional sanitary arrangements were being questioned. In the interests of "taste, decency, and propriety," the *Farmer's Almanack*, New England's most widely read publication besides the Bible, took to criticizing the prominent way in which traditional farmsteads sited their privies. Many owners of newer and larger homes began shielding their privies from sight, often disguising them in sheds attached to the house.

Although by 1800 New Englanders had commonly achieved a considerable rise in material standards compared even to Revolutionary times, their homes would strike us as dark and poorly heated, with sparse furnishings, bare floors, and unadorned walls. By the 1830s, however, the trappings of domestic refinement had begun to fill the rooms of middling as well as wealthier New England households. While this new abundance bypassed the poor and spread more slowly among families living in remote country neighborhoods, the changes were distinctly apparent in the homes of successful farmers and artisans, as well as those of prosperous merchants and professionals.

Matched sets of chairs, mass-produced in New England shops and selling for thirty to seventy-five cents apiece, were soon filling parlors and sitting rooms in increasing numbers. In more prosperous homes, cast-iron parlor stoves and cookstoves, which burned less firewood and provided more heat, were beginning to replace "old-fashioned"

Above: English transfer-printed ceramics were in universal use in New England. The image "Lafayette at the Tomb of Franklin" was enormously popular

Opposite: The most prosperous rural families could light their homes with a whale oil burning "sinumbra" lamp—so called because it was designed to light the table without casting a shadow

Above left: This c. 1832 dress is made of fabric factory woven and printed in Fall River, Massachusetts

Above right: This silk brocade dress dates to c. 1840. The pointed waist and narrow sleeves were a new fashion in women's clothing

Left: A selection of women's headwear for all occasions: a quilted bonnet (center) for chores; a collapsible "calash" (rear) for practical, everyday wear; silk and straw bonnets (left and right) for more formal occasions

hearths. Farm families continued to make their own tallow candles, but the increasing number of candlesticks in probate inventories tells us they were using more of them as standards of illumination changed. By the 1830s, center village families were replacing candles with brighter-burning whale oil lamps. The most well-to-do might illuminate their parlors with one or two of the very expensive new lamps that burned highly refined sperm oil. Both the Argand lamp, developed in 1798, and its successor the "astral lamp" provided ten times the light of a single candle. Window curtains made from newly abundant fabrics provided privacy from passers-by and created an exterior image of prosperity for many village homes. Parlor carpets and clocks, once the defining marks of elite households, became considerably more plentiful, as did images of all kinds. More prosperous village residents could have their likenesses taken by an itinerant portrait painter, another rapidly expanding trade in the 1830s. Engravings of popular heroes like George Washington, Benjamin Franklin, and Andrew Jackson sold widely as well. Even in homes that had no art on the walls there was now mass-produced English pottery decorated with "transfer printed" images of exotic scenery, public buildings, and historical events.

As keeping up with fashion became an ever more respectable preoccupation, par-

Two Children of the Morse Family depicts the clothing and trappings of a comfortable early-nineteenth-century childhood (Oil painting by William Matthew Prior, c. 1841–45)

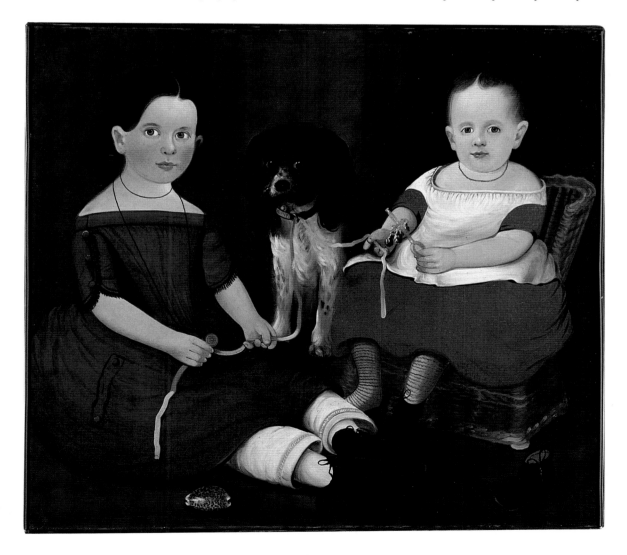

ticularly for women, the dress of both sexes was changing greatly. New England women first abandoned the wide skirts with tight waists and high necks of the late eighteenth century and for a time turned to a classically inspired "Empire" style, emphasizing slim lightweight skirts, with high waists and low-cut necklines, often white and sleeveless. But by 1820, fuller skirts had returned, with petticoats underneath, full puffed sleeves on the upper arm, neck frills, collars, and colorful prints. Fashionable headwear, from simple quilted hoods and green silk "calashes" to fine straw hats made in New England, became important features of style for well-dressed women. Milliners did a brisk business providing elaborately trimmed bonnets, as every season called for new linings, trimmings, and ribbons.

Men's clothing had also begun to change after the Revolution. Prominent waistcoats and long-tailed coats, knee breeches, and buckled shoes, gave way to long narrow-legged trousers, short vests, boots or brogans, and closely fitted coats or jackets, although farmers continued to wear their frocks and craftsmen their aprons. Cocked or low-crowned hats were abandoned in favor of tall "stovepipe" hats. New England men most often wore white shirts, although striped and even red or blue garments could be seen. Men generally wore a neck handkerchief—white, black, or colored—tied around and under the collar of the shirt. For greater formality they could don a stiff collar and neck-tie piece called a "stock." Coats and trousers came in a range of grays, browns, and blues, but merchants, professionals, and other men at their most formal tended increasingly to wear black.

Children, both boys and girls, were dressed in loose-fitting frocks from infancy until the age of three or four. Young girls were then dressed in shifts, petticoats, and gowns. And by the 1830s they might be given trouserlike "drawers" to wear under their frocks. The fashion for dressing young boys in little jacket-and-trouser combinations called "skeleton suits" gave way in the 1830s to shirts, trousers, and a long coat or "surtout." As boys and girls grew older, they donned somewhat less formal versions of their parents' attire.

All clothing, including shoes, was still cut, pieced, and sewn entirely by hand. Footwear was the province of shoemakers, whether "custom" or "sale," and most coats and greatcoats were made by tailors or tailoresses. Dressmakers and seamstresses worked for the more affluent, and only a few ready-made garments were available. For most families the bulk of the work of clothing production still fell to the women of each household. The great profusion of factory-produced textiles that had released most women from their long hours of spinning and weaving probably increased their seemingly endless labor with needle and thread. The growing ascendancy of fashion sparked exchanges of patterns, yearly alterations, and creative embellishments. Women's letters often included descriptions of new styles, fashionable colors, or important accessories.

Greater abundance and variety led to higher standards of sufficiency and "decency" in clothing, and personal wardrobes grew larger. A man would be more likely to own more than just a couple of pairs of trousers and a jacket, and a woman to have more than a couple of dresses. The formal business clothing of merchants, lawyers, and ministers could still be distinguished from the rougher working garb of farmers and craftsmen—but humbler folk had better clothes for going to meeting. And although all

Above: A man's great coat, made in Vermont between 1815 and 1840. Many men in rural New England wore such a "double-cape coat of sheep's gray," as local historian Francis Underwood remembered it. This coat has been reproduced for wear by Old Sturbridge Village interpreters

Opposite: Prosperous farmer James Bowdoin posed for his 1840 portrait in formal attire: black suit, patterned waistcoat, white shirt with high collar, and black cravat (Oil painting by David Waite Bowdoin, 1840)

the silks, crepes, and ribbons in the "Sabbathday" finery of center village women served to remind those from farm families of the inadequacies of their best gowns, they too dressed better than their mothers. Emily Farrar thought that cotton fabrics were so cheap by 1836 "that there is no excuse for any person's not being well provided." Of course, there were families in every town who saw little of the new abundance and could not afford "respectable" clothing. In fact, Ladies' Charitable Associations in many communities had assumed the task of providing poor children with clothing "sufficient to go to school and meeting."

The Fitch House

Overleaf left: The Fitch House has a homemade rose trellis to the left of the red-painted door

Overleaf right, top: The Fitch House parlor, with its trappings of gentility— shelf clock, fire frame, sofa, husband-and-wife portraits, and matched set of chairs ready for tea

Overleaf right, bottom: Imported English tableware displayed on the open dresser in the Fitch House kitchen. Increasingly available ceramics were changing the look of mealtime in New England households

Professional men, storekeepers, and tavernkeepers could always be found in the center village, along with a prosperous farmer or two, but most village households were headed by craftsmen, often called "mechanics" in the language of the nineteenth century. Usually living in the village's less imposing dwellings, they worked with their hands in small shops, producing goods for market, serving their farm family customers in the countryside, or meeting the needs of travelers along the roads. Opportunity had drawn them to the village and most were prospering in its lively economy. Some were producing goods that would be shipped great distances for sale in larger markets. Village mechanics included blacksmiths, carpenters, cabinetmakers, hatters and tailors, wheelwrights, harness makers, and tanners. There were also shoemakers, tinworkers, and printers.

The Fitch House at Old Sturbridge Village was already nearly one hundred years old when the Greek Revival styled Meetinghouse at the end of the common was built in 1832. As center villages took shape in New England, nearby farmland was usually subdivided and sold off in smaller lots, often leaving an original farmhouse and its outbuildings standing on a small village plot. This eighteenth-century dwelling, like the Fenno House next door, represents an early farmhouse long since incorporated into the growing village. With gambrel roof and ell at the rear, the "story and a loft" Fitch House is a good example of a building altered and expanded over the years. It was built in Willimantic, Connecticut, about thirty miles south of Sturbridge, as a single-room house in 1735. Three additional rooms were added later in the eighteenth century, and the ell in 1820. A farmhouse no longer, the Fitch House is presented now as the residence of a successful country printer and his growing family. To the right of the house from the road are a small barn, corn barn, and woodshed, with a large vegetable garden beyond. A colorful flower garden beside the carriage path, light yellow paint, a white picket fence, and a homemade rose trellis over the bright red door signify this family's comfort and prosperity.

The Fitch House is furnished for a busy and crowded household—including a husband and wife in their middle forties, with half a dozen children ranging in age from early childhood to late teens. The house can also accommodate a young man employed by the husband at his printing business. Although in the cities the links between workers

and their employers' households were being broken, country artisans were still likely to be feeding and lodging their apprentices and journeymen in the 1830s.

The agricultural year influenced daily life a good bit less in the center village than on outlying farms. Center village women were free from many of the burdensome chores of farming life and had more time to devote to their children, keeping the house, and keeping up with their neighbors, as well as their endless sewing. School, church, and store were much nearer, and there were many more opportunities for socializing with neighbors. With more time and money available, they began to develop a new style of life—one of increasing ambition for material comforts, aspirations to gentility, and a growing interest in community affairs, education, and fashion.

The colorful, inviting interior of the Fitch House suggests the household's emerging prosperity, invested in bright wallpapers, new paint, and window curtains. The furniture is a mix of pieces, blending the products made by local woodworkers with items made in rural New England's new chair factories and sold in retail "ware rooms." Much of the daily activity in the household takes place in a modest and comfortable sitting room, sometimes called the "family parlor," where the family usually takes its meals. But when the printer's wife entertains the ladies of the Female Charitable Society, they gather for tea in the more lavishly decorated best parlor. This room is furnished quite "genteely," with carpet, sofa, doors painted to simulate mahogany, matched portraits of

husband and wife, and an elegant parlor stove, all tidily arranged for receiving visitors.

The newest section of the house is a spacious kitchen in the ell at the back. The worktables, chairs, built-in storage, and dresser with the family's best edgeware all suggest that such a "new kitchen" would represent a modest but significant version of domestic improvement. As in most 1830s kitchens, the cooking is still done in the open fireplace. Besides pots and kettles hanging over the kitchen fire, there are the "bake kettles," which Mary Livermore remembered "for the baking of biscuit and gingerbread over beds of live coals . . ." and a reflective box of bright tinplate, called a "tin-kitchen," which was used "for the roasting of meats and poultry before the fire." The old kitchen at the Fitch House has become a bedchamber for the daughters, a storage space, and a "pass-through" or corridor.

Center village children were less likely than farm children to be needed for the household's productive work. Many nonfarming families might have agreed with Lydia Maria Child, herself a village dweller, who contended in 1831 that "it is very difficult to furnish young children with sufficient employment." Fathers went off to work at store or shop and did not usually bring their young sons along. Children's games and toys as well as schoolbooks are more in evidence in the Fitch House than in most farm dwellings; but Yankee culture valued work very highly, and few center village children were allowed to be truly idle. Young girls sewed, embroidered, helped with the housework, and cared for still smaller children, while young boys ran errands, carried firewood, and saw to the family horse and other livestock. Some, but not all, of the boys would eventually follow their fathers' trades, and the girls would seek their callings in married life. Few would go into farming or marry farmers.

The Fitch House represents the work of a printer's wife who has turned her home into a temple of domesticity—devoting her days and energies to cleaning, sewing, cooking, gardening, and the proper raising of her children. Susan Lesley remembered how her

This early hand-cranked washing machine was used in some affluent rural families who sought to reduce washday drudgery

mother, Anne Jean Lyman of Northampton, Massachusetts, "rose at dawn, threw open windows, began housecleaning. The two parlors, dining room, entry and staircase were all carefully and thoroughly swept before six o'clock." Occasionally, New England women approached their domestic chores with such dedication that the weekly laundry was already finished and the "flags of victory waving on the lines" by the time the family arose for breakfast. Most New England women found it a dreadful "pandemonium" to attempt much cooking while handling the task of washing clothes. On laundry days at the Fitch House, hardly anything else gets done all day except the hauling of water to tubs and barrels, the scrubbing, rinsing, and wringing by hand of soiled clothes and linens, and the hanging of the laundry out to dry on lines in the yard—with most of another day spent at ironing. Clothes need to be dampened and rolled, and irons heated and reheated on trivets in the fireplace. Dresses, collars and caps, men's shirts, and table linens have to be starched as well to uphold a "respectable" standard of personal appearance in the community.

Many center village women approached their community obligations and educational concerns with the same vigor they applied to household chores. Anne Jean Lyman carefully selected the prints she would hang on the walls of her house for their educational and moral value and maintained a spirited interest in reading and learning. One of her letters in 1832 described how she and an older daughter "have had a good opportunity to read this winter and to improve the children in various ways. Indeed I think winter is the season of mental improvement." In fact, shaping their children's mental and moral characters was of such importance to New England women that it led them to form hundreds of "maternal associations" for mutual support in Christian motherhood. It was also one of the most insistent themes of advice in the emerging literature on child rearing that became so popular in the 1830s.

"It is of incalculable importance that the early impressions made on the infant

Of necessity, family members in winter worked and played in close proximity

mind should . . . give a right direction to the moral character," pronounced Mary Ware Howland, herself a mother living in the center village of West Brookfield, Massachusetts, in *The Infant School Manual* she published in 1829. Such principles not only guided the establishment of little private schools for "small children," but they played a strong part in the daily home life of many families as well. "After breakfast," in the Lyman household in Northampton, "a chapter in the Bible and prayers were read." Lydia Maria Child thought children should have books, in addition to the Bible, which could "combine amusement with instruction," and she devoted a lengthy chapter in *The Mother's Book* to recommending books for children. Virtually every title that appeared on Mrs. Child's list, and more besides, could be found among the books that Mrs. Lyman kept at home. Such books were read with concentrated attention in homes like the Fitch House.

Raising children required, of course, tending not only to their physical and mental nourishment, but also to their clothing. Sewing and mending clothing, bedding, table linens, and towels for the family were never-ending tasks. There are constant references to sewing and mending family clothes in Mrs. Lyman's letters, echoing those in the letters, diaries, and recollections of New England mothers and daughters. Pamela Brown of Plymouth Notch, Vermont, spent a typical December day in 1835 sewing with her sister: "Louisa and I finished my cloak. Mother went to Cavendish. I think some of going to Senica Carter's wedding. I made Marcia's babe a bonnet and Louisa made me one." Advice books never failed to recommend that mothers teach daughters to sew their own clothes and that young women be certain to master both plain and fancy sewing. "A woman who does not know how to sew," pronounced *The Young Lady's Friend*, "is as defi-

ELIZABETH . F. CURTIS

Above left: A "Fashion Plate" engraving from Godey's Lady's Book

Above right: A "theorem painting" by a nine-year-old girl. Instruction in such decorative work was a frequent part of female education

Right: Bonnets and trimmings surround a Village milliner intent on her work

cient in her education as a man who does not know how to write." One woman in Bellingham, Massachusetts, was as pleased with her four-year-old daughter's sewing as with her early progress at learning the alphabet: "She has learned to sew very neatly, all of her own accord, and has already made herself quite useful."

The Fitch House also portrays the life of women, so numerous in rural New England, who combined genteel aspirations with practical labor. When they are sewing, the women in the Fitch House move from window to window, seeking the best available light. Sometimes they stitch shoe uppers that will ultimately be bottomed at

the shoe shop, an 1830s strategy to earn some extra cash. Now and again they work on a fancy bit of embroidery to embellish some garment or accessory. At other times, they sew plain but "decent" clothes of the sort that charitable societies of the 1830s gave to needy families.

Sharing the sitting room with other family members, a milliner can often be found in the Fitch House making stylish 1830s bonnets. More than any other woman's trade, the milliner's combined hard work and gentility in equal measure. No women in the countryside had greater need to keep pace with the changes of fashion. Beginning with stiff buckram shapes, Village milliners mold them to the contours once prescribed by the fashions of Boston, New York, London, and Paris. With exacting craftsmanship they cover, line, and decorate the bonnets with silk, crepe, feathers, and ribbons.

Millinery in the early nineteenth century was custom work; each bonnet would have been made to order after careful consultation with the purchaser. After 1836, milliners usually worked with a recent copy of *Godey's Lady's Book* as well. This periodical was edited by Sara Josepha Hale, a New England woman who earlier had turned to sewing and writing to support herself and her young children after the death of her husband. *Godey's* was the first successful and widely read American magazine for women. It featured stories, poetry, and serious essays, but it was also the bible of women's fashion, providing lavish color plates that were indispensable to country dressmakers and milliners.

The Fitch House printer and his wife are portrayed as committed members of the Congregational Church and active participants in rural New England's growing network of voluntary associations. Female Charitable Societies organized women to sew for the poor. Town lyceums expressed New Englanders' enthusiasm for self-improvement by presenting debates and public lectures on "history, art, science, and public questions." Seashells in the family parlor from the far-off Pacific Ocean are evidence of a third—missionary societies. By the 1830s, rural New Englanders were supporting their compatriots working as Christian missionaries in Oregon, the Near East, and especially the Sandwich Islands (now Hawaii). Rural churches organized groups to send them books, clothes, and furnishings. In return, grateful missionary families often sent back exotic gifts, such as seashells. They were displayed in many a New England home as proud symbols of a family's dedication to the causes of Christianity and civilization.

A c. 1820 portrait of Salem Towne, Sr., for whom the Village's Salem Towne House was built in 1796 (Oil painting by Francis Alexander, c. 1820)

The Salem Towne House

From the east end of the Common at Old Sturbridge Village, directly opposite the Meetinghouse, the elegant Salem Towne House exerts a graceful mastery over the aspirations of Center Village society. In the 1830s, it was the home of the family of Salem Towne, Jr., of Charlton, Massachusetts, about eight miles east of Sturbridge, who inherited the house at the death of his father in 1825. Both father and son were enterprising farmers, surveyors, and men of business. They took the lead in the affairs of their town

A detail of the Towne House front doorway, with triangular pediment and fanlight over the door—a design taken directly from an English guidebook of 1794

and church, and were central figures in the local economy. In a letter of 1823, Salem spoke of the elder Towne as "the best of fathers." Like his father, he went on to become a pillar of the Congregational Church, a justice of the peace, and a major general of the Massachusetts militia. Prosperous farmers like the Townes, along with other influential families—those of lawyers, bankers, doctors, and merchants—were primarily responsible for bringing new ideas of fashion and refinement to the countryside. Their handsome dwellings were commonly found in prominent center village locations.

The balanced proportions and refined details of this substantial house clearly distinguish it as the work of a skillful country builder. Its symmetrical two-chimney plan, fanlight above the front entrance, and spacious central hallway all reflect the influence of the Federal style, largely derived from the work of the Scottish architect Robert Adam. Rural carpenters were beginning to interpret and adapt elements of the style when the Salem Towne House was built in 1796. The transition was only just under way, however, and traces of earlier building traditions—four different doorway designs for each of the house's sides and the Palladian window at the stair landing—are still evident in the Towne House's design.

Housewright Samuel Stetson combined the training he received in his coastal hometown of Scituate, Massachusetts, with ideas from architectural pattern books to create a number of "mansion houses" in central Massachusetts, including one for his Charlton neighbor Salem Towne. Stetson drew many of the Towne House's design elements from William Pain's English guidebooks for carpenters, *The Practical Builder*, published in an American edition in 1792, and *The Builder's Pocket Treasure*, available in 1794. Virtually all the details of finish in the house—the windows, cornices, overmantels, and moldings—can be found in Pain's illustrations. The design of the front entry, with its half-round fanlight, triangular pediment, and half-round columns, was borrowed from Pain as well, as was a chimney piece in the southwest parlor. Within and without, using elements selected and rearranged from Pain's designs, the Towne House was built to impress its visitors.

Overleaf: *The gazebo and formal garden at the Towne House. Decorative horticulture was of great interest to many progressive farmers and their wives*

In the Village, the Towne House is portrayed as the headquarters of a large and flourishing farm fronting on the Common. On its north side, the house is flanked by a farmyard with substantial outbuildings, an orchard, and the Cider Mill. To the south is a formal garden with walkways, a grape arbor, and a gazebo. The garden's layout of symmetrical flower beds—with colorful tulips, baptisia and peonies, marigolds and old roses—reflects the growing interest of many prosperous New England families in ornamental horticulture. The house and its surroundings typify the rural landscape created by an affluent, progressive New England farmer, and illustrate the wide-ranging activities of his busy household.

Salem and Sally Spurr Towne were the heads of their well-to-do establishment but at times still worked alongside their hired help as they managed the farm, dairy, and house. In 1830, according to the federal census schedules, thirteen people—including seven of their nine children and three hired men, one of whom was African-American—were living in the Towne household, making it the largest in Charlton.

The surviving Towne family papers provide intriguing clues about life in a prosperous rural household, but they are incomplete. To provide a fuller picture, the museum undertook a study of comparable families, finding the Ward family of Shrewsbury, Massachusetts, about twenty miles northeast of Sturbridge, in particular, shared many characteristics with the Townes. The two families were strikingly similar, not only in the size and make-up of their households, but also in their wealth, scale of farming, religious affiliation, and political activities. Combined with the Towne records, the Wards' voluminous letters, diaries, and accounts allow a far more detailed interpretation of daily life in the Salem Towne House and others like it.

Based on these sources, we may imagine the house on a typical winter day in 1830: Three men were outside cutting firewood, spreading manure, or sowing winter rye, while Salem Towne, Jr., was working in the sitting room he sometimes used as an office, settling accounts, negotiating a land purchase, or witnessing legal documents; his wife, Sally, was attending a meeting of the Female Charitable Society; the family's oldest daughter, like many young women of twenty, was away on an extended visit with relatives in New Hampshire; her seventeen-year-old sister was caring for her youngest brother and sister, ages one and three, by herself, while the four middle children, a young

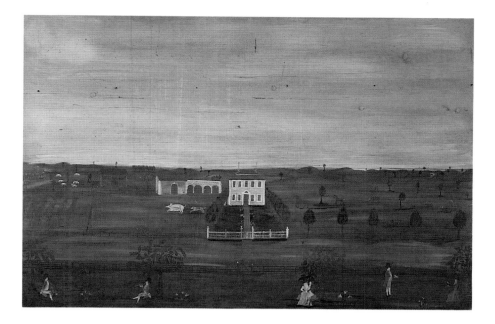

Right: This overmantel painting, depicting a gentleman farmer's house and grounds, came from the now demolished Jennings house in Brookfield, Massachusetts. The small barn and carriage shed shown in the painting served as a model for the reconstruction of the Towne House outbuildings. It has since been discovered that both houses had the same builder

Below: The elegant and symmetrical front facade of the Towne House— deeply impressive in a country setting

boy and three girls, were at the center village's district school; a hired woman carried on with her busy rounds of housework, cooking, and mending.

On another day, Salem Towne, Jr., might have been found in his working clothes assigning "stints" of work to his hired hands, helping them butcher a steer for the family larder, or selecting livestock to be taken to the great Brighton market outside Boston.

Perhaps preparations were afoot for an upcoming business trip to Boston or a journey to manage timberlands in Maine. His oldest son, reading law in Worcester, was expected home on one of the two daily stages. Sally, with her two older daughters and the hired woman, had already packed four youngsters off to school, swept and dusted, then cooked, served, and cleared away breakfast and dinner. Finally, all the while tending to the needs of an infant and toddler, they had turned their attentions to the work of the dairy. In the evening, after supper and family prayers, members of this busy household—and others like it—wrote letters, updated accounts, practiced lessons, embroidered, read aloud to one another, or sang to the music of the pianoforte.

The house and its furnishings reflect the tastes and interests of the prosperous parents of a large family and the bustling life that they oversaw. There are four rooms on each of its two floors, on either side of a wide carpeted hallway—a formal design that sets this dwelling apart from the museum's other residences. The furnishings in the house would likewise have been elegant and expensive by the standards of the countryside. A few of those currently displayed have a history of ownership by the Towne family, but most have been chosen to illustrate typical practice in the decoration of fashionable country homes in the 1830s. The house's hallway and parlor carpets and its wide variety of wallpapers have been reproduced from documented originals found in early-nineteenth-century settings. Most of the wallpapers are English and French patterns that were being imported by New England merchants, but the blue paper in the bedchamber over the kitchen is American-made. Some of the woven carpets are also products of a new and expanding American industry, supplying a growing demand by 1830 and protected by high tariffs. From teacups to cookstove, the house reflects the characteristic choices of a family like the Townes, combining imports with fine goods made in New England and putting together items that might have passed down through the family with the later fashions of the 1820s and 1830s.

In the sitting room, there is a mahogany secretary desk where the man of the house can conduct farm and financial business, while the Sheraton-style lady's worktable suggests that a wife and daughters would sew or knit in this room, storing their projects in its capacious interior. Household members might gather here in the evening to recount the day's endeavors and amusements, write letters, or read. In the parlor at the front of the house, there is an imported Brussels carpet on the floor, and newly popular "swag and tail" curtains adorn the windows. The upholstered mahogany Sheraton-style sofa and Hepplewhite side chairs are arranged formally around the walls, following traditional practice. The new and fashionable Empire-style table is displayed in the center of the room, where it can hold a lamp or be used for serving tea. This most formal room would have been used for important visitors and elegant entertaining and have witnessed weddings and funerals.

The square pianoforte in the parlor is an example of the early nineteenth century's most conspicuous icon of affluence and refinement. The Village's figured mahogany and rosewood veneer instrument was made by John Osborn in the early 1820s when he was working at his address in "Boston near Boylston Market," and a bill of sale links it to the family. Music was an important part of the Towne family tradition, and in letters home Salem often mentioned his daughter Sally's piano playing. "Sally must play the Foaming Billows when I am crossing the lake," he imagined while traveling in New Hampshire, and, during a long stay managing investments in Maine, he thought Sally might be "playing Days of Absence, but will soon play Pa's return." Two volumes of young Sally's sheet music for piano—waltzes, military marches, parlor ballads, and Irish melodies—are in the museum's Research Library, and they still provide selections for occasional performances of music in the parlor at the Towne House.

Opposite the formal parlor at the Towne House is another elegant room furnished for dining. It aims for a "substantial" effect, following the standards of contemporary decorating advice, with a painted canvas floor cloth, eighteenth-century engravings, and an ironstone dinner service made in England in the 1820s. A portrait of Salem Towne, Sr., painted around 1820 when he was in his late seventies, hangs over the fireplace.

The bedchambers upstairs, in New England often named in reference to the room beneath, are furnished to reflect the presence of the various members of this large household in the 1830s. The sitting room chamber is furnished as the room occupied by Salem and Sally and their infant son. There are bed and window hangings of white cotton dimity and an elegant gilded dressing table made in Boston between 1815 and 1825. The New England–made fancy Sheraton side chairs can be moved to more public rooms when needed for entertaining. At the front of the house the two rooms are furnished as bedchambers for the Towne daughters and female visitors, with two or three persons sleeping in each bed. Removable partitions make it clear that these spaces could be joined to create a ballroom or large meeting room. Salem Towne, Sr., hosted monthly meetings of the local Masonic lodge here until 1806, and the family retained its painted wall decorations depicting the Cedars of Lebanon.

One of these chambers also provides a convenient site for a quilting frame. Francis Underwood remembered his mother's country neighbors arriving for a "quiltin" dressed in their "best gowns, cambric collars, and lace caps." They sat around the quilt-

Page 148, top left: The center table set for tea amid the formal elegance of the Towne House's parlor

Page 148, top right: A portrait of Salem Towne, Jr., overlooks the sideboard in the entry hall of the Towne House (Oil painting by Francis Alexander, c. 1820)

Page 148, bottom: A meeting of the Ladies Charitable Society in the Towne House sitting room

Page 149, top: The sitting room chamber at the Towne House with canopied infant's crib and parents' bed

Page 149, bottom: Set for a formal meal, the dining table in the Towne House displays a service of English ironstone that would have been sumptuous by rural standards

Pages 150–51: A James No. 2 Patent Cookstove, modern kitchen technology for the 1830s, occupies the center of the Towne House kitchen

ing frame, chatting about their neighbors and comparing opinions on a host of topics while stitching together the intricate patchwork patterns of a quilt for one of the party. Such occasions, including the adjournment for afternoon tea (a substantial meal in the early nineteenth century), brought women together in the 1830s, but center village women were just as likely to be sewing the quilt for some charitable purpose as for one of their own households. Some had become sober occasions indeed—the bylaws of a few

The ballroom/front bedchamber of the Towne House; its walls retain their original "Cedars of Lebanon" painted decorations

sewing circles and charitable societies forbade chatting, gossip, and tea in favor of "conversation as becomes the Gospel."

Male guests and relatives might have slept in the kitchen chamber with the Townes' sons, or in the garret, lit by the windows of the monitor roof, with the hired hands. In the early nineteenth century, French bedsteads, like the one shown in the kitchen chamber, were recommended for domestic use and considered suitable "either for servants or children to sleep upon."

The kitchen floor is covered with a layer of fresh sand to illustrate a characteristic way of keeping bare floors clean in early New England. The sand, spread on after the floor is scrubbed, absorbs drips and spills and mud tracked in from outside. An energetic and fastidious housewife would end her day's work by disposing of the old sand and sweeping new sand into elegant geometrical patterns to await the morning. The kitchen also displays an important innovation in household technology: the fireplace has been bricked up and a hole cut into the chimney to accommodate a cast-iron cookstove. It is an example of America's first domestic appliance; this one is a James Patent Stove, which came in eight sizes at various prices. Widely advertised as making cooking easier, supplying more heat, and saving on fuel, cookstoves and parlor stoves were introduced to the countryside in the 1820s, beginning in prosperous households like the Townes'. Because the small ovens on early cookstoves were often unreliable, housewives frequently chose to keep open the old brick oven in the fireplace—a decision this kitchen reflects.

The rooms below the kitchen stairs were added to the original house after it was moved to Old Sturbridge Village. The lower kitchen, with its large open hearth, has been reserved for rougher, messier work—doing the family laundry and cleaning all the equipment and utensils used in milking, buttermaking, and cheese production. In the adjacent dairy room there is a "self-regulating, patent" cheese press, one of the technical improvements that sparked the interest of progressive farmers in the 1830s. It promised to take some of the guesswork out of cheesemaking. A door from the lower kitchen opens onto the Townes' farmyard, with its stone-walled enclosures, large barn, milking stalls, and sheep sheds.

The Parsonage

The Parsonage

Ordinary rural New Englanders did not take to painting their houses until the early years of the nineteenth century. Before that time, most country dwellings were simply left unpainted, weathering to a shade they usually called "brown." The imposing homes of the well-to-do were, in sharp contrast, painted white, yellow, "stone-colour," or occasionally red. And eighteenth-century rural meetinghouses were often distinguished by vivid hues, including accents of sky blue, pumpkin orange, chocolate brown, and pea green. But as center villages emerged, white became the dominant color for meetinghouses and homes alike, reflecting a taste for simplicity, order, and increasing uniformity in the landscape. In the 1830s, a mid-eighteenth-century lean-to house on the town common would most likely have been painted white to harmonize with the more modern structures around it.

Housewright Thomas Bannister built a typical lean-to house "on speculation" in 1748 in the country neighborhood of "Podunk" in East Brookfield, Massachusetts, about ten miles north of Sturbridge, and sold it to the farmer Solomon Richardson. By the time Old Sturbridge Village acquired the house nearly two centuries later, some windows and room arrangements had been altered, and parts of the structure had fallen into disrepair. However, the basic features of its design remained largely unchanged, including its "two-over-two" house form, with two finished bedchambers upstairs over two rooms below, a steeply sloping roof creating a large kitchen space at the rear, and a graceful doorway. Today, it is presented as the 1830s home of a Congregational minister and his family. To recognize its early-nineteenth-century museum identity, this house is now called the Parsonage.

Up through the mid-nineteenth century, parsonages were private dwellings. Ministers' families had to buy or rent their own houses, since local churches had not yet begun to provide them. Village historians have estimated that a house like this would have cost $600 to $800 around 1830, so that a family settling into such a parsonage would likely have paid rent at the rate of about $50 to $65 a year, or have made annual mortgage payments of about $100 to $160 on a five-year loan. Such costs were not quite the implausible bargains they might seem, however, for the yearly salaries of Massachusetts country ministers in 1830 averaged no more than $500—usually payable at the end of the year.

At these levels of support, many Congregational ministers, serving New England's largest and historically dominant church, found it a struggle to provide both the spiritual and social leadership that the community expected. In addition to maintaining a genteel residence, a ministerial family had heavy expenses: a horse and chaise for paying calls; books and periodicals for theological study; highly respectable but not ostentatious furniture and clothes; entertainment for a steady stream of visitors and overnight guests.

Supplying at least one item of ministerial expense—firewood—was part of New England's communal tradition. Most congregations contracted to deliver a quantity of firewood to their minister as part of his annual support. Parishioners often

turned the "minister's wood-spell," as they called it, into a yearly ceremony. In Ashby, Massachusetts, the Reverend Ezekiel Bascom's congregation delivered an astounding forty cords on New Year's Day in 1824. His wife Ruth noted in her diary that many people came by to visit or simply stopped "to view the great load of wood," before some fifty men arrived the following week to cut and stack it. By the 1830s, these abundant wood-spells had not disappeared but they were less common. Some ministers complained of tardy delivery or of not enough wood to last through the season, and many had to cut it up themselves. In March of 1833, clergyman Thomas Robbins was happy to record that his society had "voted me a kind donation of three cords of wood," but at other times he was obliged to purchase firewood at rates ranging from $6 to $9 per cord.

Congregational ministers of the eighteenth century were expected to stay for a lifetime in the parish that called them, and their influence and authority in the community were unrivaled. By the early nineteenth century, they had lost much of their security and some of their authority. On the average, ministers now stayed only five or six years in one place before moving on. Congregations saw ministers as employees who might be dismissed, not lifetime leaders. Clergymen had begun to think of their work as a career, a sequence of steps that might lead to employment at a succession of churches, missionary work, or even college teaching. Ministers—and their wives—were still

powerful moral and social leaders in the 1830s, but their beliefs and conduct were subject to the constant scrutiny and comment of parishioners.

At the same time, clergymen's duties were more demanding than ever before. Besides preparing two lengthy sermons each week, ministers visited widely throughout their towns, counseled the troubled, attended to funerals, and solemnized marriages. They were expected to take an active role in education and nonpolitical community affairs. Many served as members of district school committees, and some took a young student or two as boarders while tutoring them—in Latin and Greek—for college admission.

The garret at the Parsonage shows a characteristic sleeping space for children. The two beds will hold four or even more

One of the downstairs rooms at the Parsonage has been fitted out as the minister's study, where he would prepare his sermons and confer with callers. The study's crowded bookshelves hold what would likely be the most extensive library in town, and there is a representative clutter of letters, pamphlets, and books on the writing table. The reform causes of 1830s America—temperance, prison reform, foreign missions, anti-slavery—called strongly to many New England ministers. They often campaigned for these causes in their communities, sometimes risking their pulpits in the process. The literature on the writing table testifies as well to another imperative—the need to create a religious revival in the community to bring sinners to salvation.

Clergymen traveled frequently, "exchanging pulpits" with neighboring congregations and attending the monthly and yearly conferences of an increasingly organized profession. The small travel desk in the minister's study allows for reading and writing away from home, with room for papers, quills, ink, and blotting sand. There is even a small box of floating "tapers," thin corks with wicks that will float on a small amount of lamp oil and serve as convenient travel lamps.

A minister and his wife could expect to receive a daily stream of visitors, men and women stopping by to receive spiritual counsel, argue theology, discuss neighborhood disputes, or organize local charities. The management of all this gracious hospitality—serving tea to guests and hosting meetings of women's associations and other social and religious groups—fell upon the shoulders of the minister's wife. In addition, she was expected to go beyond "the narrow circle of her domestic concerns," to be a paragon of womanly knowledge, spirituality, and moral strength.

Frequent overnight guests in the parsonage added to the pressures on wives hoping for more time to attend to the needs of their families. Ministers' households traditionally provided hospitality for respectable travelers, especially the wives and daughters of other ministers, so they could avoid staying in taverns. The diary of minister's wife Ruth Henshaw Bascom records how she coped with serving the regular members of her household along with a continuing parade of visitors: In one month in 1825, the Bascoms had people "lodged overnight" on five separate occasions, received nineteen afternoon callers, and entertained fifteen extra people at dinner and seventeen at supper. The women who ran such households often found the endless domestic labors that supported this sociability to be exhausting, and eagerly looked forward to help from visiting relatives—mothers, sisters, or cousins.

A door in the parents' bedchamber at the Village's Parsonage opens to an unfinished attic space above the kitchen, a place where children usually slept. Two low beds, enough to sleep four or even six, plus a few toys and belongings, are tucked neatly under the rafters of the lean-to roof. Like most attics, this one is filled with a mixed assortment of household belongings. In the summer, it holds unused andirons brought up and wrapped in newspaper, while a "fireboard" closes off the empty hearth below. In the winter, the fireboard is hauled upstairs to share the space with the squashes and pumpkins, and garden-grown herbs and onions hanging from the rafters. A spinning wheel, long out of use in the household, has been relegated to the attic for storage. In a corner near the narrow back stairs stands a barrel, almost full of donated goods being prepared for shipment to the "mission field." Country parsonages were the headquarters of hundreds of missionary societies that linked New England to "Hindustan" or the Sandwich Islands.

As late as 1800, many ministers, such as Samuel Goodrich's father in Ridgefield, Connecticut, "carried on the farm, besides attending to other parochial duties." By the 1830s, ministers' families were much more likely just to keep chickens and tend their vegetable gardens. The gardens at the Parsonage are exemplary, planted in up-to-date raised beds, a practice the minister's wife could read about in a progressive horticultural publication like Thomas Bridgeman's *Kitchen Gardener's Assistant*. Besides the peas, potatoes, and carrots, grown in every country garden because they are "good keepers," there are other vegetables, recommended for the newly recognized benefits of eating them fresh—asparagus, lettuce, spinach, tomatoes, and eggplant.

Summer mornings at the Parsonage often find an interpreter portraying the minister or his wife—if not a visiting relative or overnight guest—out in the flower-filled dooryard. Visitors stopping by at that time are invited inside for an inclusive and lively tour of the house, where dramatic role-playing performances bring the bustling hospitality of an 1830s minister's household to life again. Callers arriving in the afternoon can visit casually with interpreters, explore the house, and examine the furnishings just as they might do at any other dwelling in the village. All who come, however, catch some strong sense of what the Parsonage is all about: balancing a devoted concern for the spiritual life of the community with the expectations of parishioners and the needs of the minister's own family.

New Dimensions of Professional Life

In the opening decade of the nineteenth century, the lives of rural professional men still had much in common with those of farmers and artisans. Not only country merchants and tradesmen, but many ministers and lawyers as well, retained a part-time involvement with farming. Work and household life were becoming more separate for most professionals, but only gradually. Although physicians generally treated patients at their homes, they, along with lawyers, usually set up offices in their houses or in small buildings on their property. Ministers counseled parishioners and prepared sermons in their studies at home, and many "sociable" obligations were given over to the household duties of their wives.

Traditionally, professionals trained for their work in the same ways artisans acquired their trades. They learned on the job, under the guidance of a practitioner willing to act as master or preceptor. After college, an aspiring Congregational minister studied for two years with a clergyman—reading theology, studying the Bible, writing sermons, and visiting parishioners. Law students apprenticed for up to five years, or only three if they had a college education. The quality of these apprenticeships, like those for mechanics, could vary considerably. A scrupulous preceptor who enjoyed teaching would guide his students carefully; a careless one might assign them only menial tasks and leave them to learn the rudiments on their own.

American society grew in complexity and the professions did as well. Training grew more formal and standards more exacting. Divinity schools were founded to teach subjects essential to the ministry, partly because college education had lost much of its theological character. As the new nation took shape, law schools and medical schools appeared, offering academic instruction to supplement traditional preceptorial teaching. County, and then state, bar associations exercised a gradually expanding influence over the professional practice of their members, and newly formed medical societies began to press for voluntary regulations and improved qualifications for physicians.

Law Office

The small one-room building near the Common, between the Parsonage and the Asa Knight Store, is a law office, erected by a country lawyer to keep his work separate from the bustle of household activities. This unassuming structure, with its plastered walls, bookshelves, storage closets, and small fireplace, links the New England countryside to the powerful and expanding enterprise of nineteenth-century American law. Built in 1796 by John McClellan of Woodstock, Connecticut, it is furnished to reflect the working world of a rural practitioner in the 1830s. In such buildings country lawyers consulted the state statutes and court reports, drafted legal documents and correspondence, and met with their clients.

At the outbreak of the Revolution, not a single edition of American law reports had appeared. The only published texts were on English common law, and a lawyer who wanted formal training had to study in England. By the 1830s, however, a distinctively American legal system had come into being, with law schools and a rapidly expanding legal literature. Much like the ingenious mechanics who "borrowed" English technology to create a new world of industry, American lawyers and jurists recast the precepts of the common law to accommodate a new society.

Law was a far more powerful profession early in the nineteenth century than it had been before the Revolution. Mid-eighteenth-century Massachusetts, for example, had had no more than one lawyer for every eight thousand people. In 1830, there was one for every eleven hundred, reflecting an increasingly complex and litigious society. In city and countryside alike, lawyers were coming to play a leading role in politics and other aspects of public life.

John McClellan came to the law in a way typical of his post-Revolutionary generation. He attended district school and was then tutored for college by local clergymen. After graduating from Yale, he studied law with local practitioners before his admission to the bar. Most lawyers practicing in the 1830s still trained in a way that was tradi-

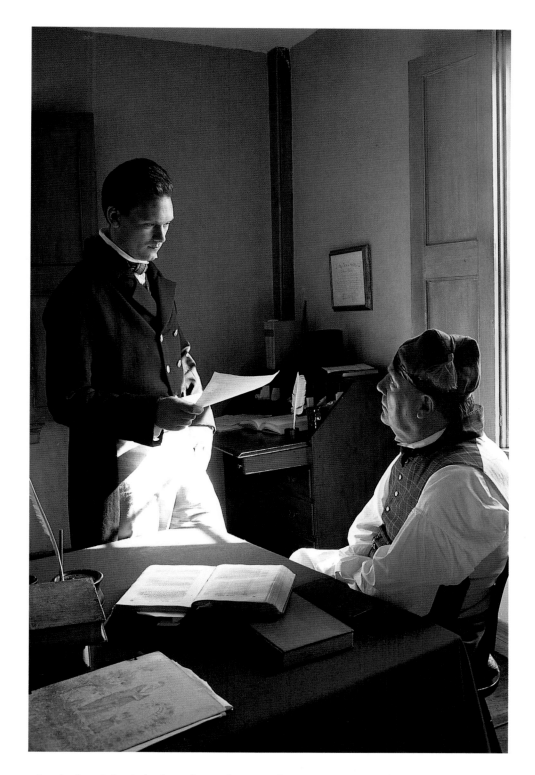

tional: they joined the bar after a three- to five-year apprenticeship in the office of an established practitioner, copying documents and reading the classic works of English common law. Young New England men preparing for a legal career in the 1820s and 1830s had an alternative, however. They could attend one of the recently established law schools—Harvard (1815) was the best known—and serve just one year of apprenticeship.

Rural lawyers usually found their way into local leadership, political office, and sometimes state government. McClellan followed a representative path: he was active in the local Temperance Society and the county Peace Society, an officer in the Pomfret Agricultural Society, a brigadier in the militia, and a justice of the peace. He served several terms in the state legislature, and every four years cast one of Connecticut's electoral votes.

Country lawyers periodically traveled to the county seat to record documents or try cases at the courthouse. These court times were often social occasions as well, when lawyers socialized with fellow members of the profession from their county or even elsewhere in the state. Despite their obligation to act as adversaries, the attorneys—as McClellan recalled—often "appeared and acted like a band of brothers."

But for all their learning and prestige, rural lawyers were still tradesmen of a kind, whose tools were writs and statute books. They drew up wills and leases, property deeds and mortgages. They advised clients about business partnerships. And because the rural economy was based on credit and exchange, they spent much—sometimes most—of their time collecting debts. As much as anyone in town, they knew the community's secrets.

At its most local level, law and justice was a very informal affair. Cases of petty crime and minor civil disputes were handled by justices of the peace, sometimes without the involvement of lawyers at all. Appointed for each town by the governor of the state, these lay judges were men like Salem Towne, Sr., and Jr., widely respected in their communities, but usually without legal training. They conducted hearings in any convenient location, often in their own parlors, and their jurisdiction covered the frictions of everyday life—small debts and commercial disputes, accusations of drunkenness or illegal gaming, even claims for the support of illegitimate children. Justices were also examining magistrates, who could send more serious cases on to the county courts for trial. These proceedings, documented in justices' record books, are regularly re-created at Old Sturbridge Village. Plaintiffs or prosecutors and defendants make their statements, call witnesses, and cross-examine. Then, as visitors watch, the justice, whether a learned lawyer or affable farmer, renders his judgment.

Thompson Bank

The Doric columns of the Thompson Bank proclaim the taste and ambition of the prosperous farmers, merchants, and professional men who invested in it. The building was designed to give a powerful impression of stability and security to its shareholders and customers. The bank was chartered in Thompson, Connecticut, about fifteen miles southeast of Sturbridge, in 1833. Capital was raised by selling shares of its stock, and construction on the building started soon afterward. Built in the Greek Revival style enormously popular in New England in the 1830s, it is remarkably monumental for such a small structure. The massive columns and bold parapet across the top, finished with sandstone-colored paint, create a miniature temple of commerce.

The building served as a bank until 1893 and remained in Thompson another seventy years before it was carefully crated up and moved to the Village. The interior has been restored to its appearance in the late 1830s. The furnishings are expensive and up-to-date. A cast-iron stove topped with classical columns repeats the Greek Revival motif, and a highly accurate "regulator" clock of Simon Willard's design accompanies a pair of fashionable and bright-burning "astral" lamps. The granite-walled vault, where currency, notes and valuable documents were stored, is safeguarded by a massive iron door; and the counter, cashier's desk, and president's office seem to welcome the arrival of dependable patrons.

The Thompson Bank was one of New England's growing number of rural commercial banks, loaning money to merchants and manufacturers in the countryside. In an expanding economy with major needs for working capital, country banks became, along with the private lending of wealthy citizens, important sources of credit. Likely borrowers would include tin or shoe manufacturers needing to purchase raw materials, storekeepers needing to finance their new spring merchandise, or a textile factory owner seeking to buy more machines. A local printer might apply for a loan in order to buy the paper, type, and ink needed to print a large edition of schoolbooks. Using the books to be printed or office equipment as collateral for his promissory note, the printer would repay the full value of the loan when due—usually in two to six months. Because the interest (typically at an annual rate of 5 to 6 percent) was deducted or "discounted" in advance from the loan amount, the loans were usually called "discounts."

Each borrower received the bank's own privately engraved notes, signed by the cashier and president, which could be used as cash. In fact, most of the money in circulation in New England was in the form of bank notes only lightly backed up by paid-in shares, but widely supported by public confidence. Bank notes were not only convenient but, in the eyes of most New England businessmen, necessary. There would be no federally issued paper money until the Civil War, and coins were simply inadequate to meet the growing scale of the economy. Oddly enough, New Englanders were actually more accustomed to handling foreign currency than their own. Until gold was discovered in California in 1848, the production of coins by the United States Mint was insufficient. Most people reckoned and settled accounts in American decimal currency, established in 1793, but dealt with a perplexing variety of foreign coins—largely Mexican and South American, but also French, English, and Dutch. *Ready Reckoners* were popular guides to this maze of currency values used by bank cashiers, storekeepers, and hard-bargaining farmwives.

Sadly, the records of the Thompson Bank itself have not survived. But in the ledgers, daybooks, cashbooks, discount books, and director's records of other New England country banks, the museum has found abundant documentation of the surprisingly intricate world of country banking. Each country bank served several adjacent towns, financing the great majority of enterprises that were too distant or small to interest city bankers. When investors petitioned the state for a bank charter, they often noted the benefit the bank would bring to communities whose citizens were inconvenienced by having to travel great distances to borrow money. Once the charter was issued, the bank was organized, with shares of stock sold to people who wanted to put their sur-

plus funds to work. Each bank was overseen by a board of directors, but usually its only full-time employee was a cashier. He kept the directors informed about the bank's activities, met with customers, reviewed loan applications with the president, conducted the bank's extensive relationships with its "correspondent" banks, and kept the books. Often a prominent member of the community, the cashier was well-paid for his judgment, discretion, and mastery of the books. He kept the now-legendary "banker's hours," opening for business sometime in the morning and closing for most of the afternoon. In reality, he worked far harder than this suggests, since the great bulk of his work was behind the scenes, holding meetings and servicing accounts.

As commercial lending institutions, country banks only offered short-term loans. Although they would often renew loans for up to several months, banks were generally unwilling to tie up funds for longer periods. Consequently, early-nineteenth-century New England farmers and others turned for mortgages—longer-term loans secured by

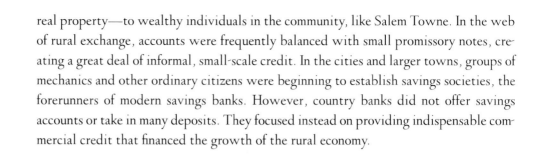

real property—to wealthy individuals in the community, like Salem Towne. In the web of rural exchange, accounts were frequently balanced with small promissory notes, creating a great deal of informal, small-scale credit. In the cities and larger towns, groups of mechanics and other ordinary citizens were beginning to establish savings societies, the forerunners of modern savings banks. However, country banks did not offer savings accounts or take in many deposits. They focused instead on providing indispensable commercial credit that financed the growth of the rural economy.

MORTGAGING THE FARM.

It is the first _ oh dash it from thy lips _   See shame and sin and death to him who sips,

Look down _ what lies beneath its sparkling foam?   And wife and helpless babes bereft of home.

CHAPTER SEVEN

Community

NEW ENGLAND WAS REMARKABLE FOR ITS DIS-tinctive institutions of community that drew each town's people together for socializing, trade, learning, worship, and debate. "All the people are neighbors," wrote New England's own Timothy Dwight, who "converse; feel; sympathize; mingle minds; cherish sentiments; and are subjects of at least some degree of refinement." New Englanders' strong sense of identity was formed not only by bonds of kinship, neighboring, and local exchange, but by their commitments to institutions of government, education, religious observance, and voluntary action.

From every New England country household, strands of the social web spread out to neighbors' dwellings, on to the district school, and to the center village with its meetinghouses, stores, and taverns. Men and women chatted with their neighbors along the road or in the kitchens, journeyed out for business and visits, attended Sunday meeting, went to funerals or stopped over to nurse the sick, learned their notes at singing school, or swelled the crowd at the Fourth of July celebration. They reaffirmed ancestral values and adjusted to changing realities as they gathered to gossip, bargain, deliberate, or pray. And they chided and exhorted one another, joked and argued, danced and sang.

Although rural people spent most of their days hard at work, they also found odd moments, often in the evenings or at the week's end, to socialize. Most farming folk visited and traded with their neighbors at least weekly, and Lyndon Freeman remembered how common it was for women of his Massachusetts town to visit "from house to house, to take tea and enjoy a social afternoon." Young Pamela Brown of Plymouth, Vermont, received guests constantly, and often went out calling herself. "Had one of the best visits I ever had in my life," she wrote in her diary after one full November day in 1836 when

Opposite: Mortgaging the Farm, one of the many engravings that brought the temperance message home to thousands of New England households

Above: Pallbearers carry the black-draped coffin to the Center Meetinghouse for the funeral sermon

Farmers with their ox teams stop to talk
as paths cross in the center village

she and Mrs. Moore "called at Mrs. Kimball's and at Mrs. Hubbard's" before taking Mrs. Slack along to call at Mr. Earle's.

Visiting with friends or kin, and then staying overnight, or "tarrying," was one of the most common of New England's social rituals. Visiting and return travel both took time, and it was often not possible to combine them on the same day even if the trip was only several miles across town. People frequently traveled in the morning, hoping to arrive at midday in time for dinner, or at least by teatime in the evening, and then spent the night. Although plans to "tarry" might occasionally be made by letter, most visitors simply arrived unannounced. Both children and adults were used to sharing beds in improvised sleeping arrangements, and well-managed households were prepared to feed a half-dozen guests at any time.

It was a long-standing New England tradition for neighbors to come together often to complete some task, great or small, and to socialize and celebrate. Groups of women gathered at quilting parties, "spinning frolics," and sewing circles, or prepared the apple harvest at "paring bees." The women talked and gossiped while they worked, and then adjourned in the late afternoon for tea. When the frolic or quilting was organized by young women of courting age, young men were invited to come by afterward for dancing or games. Several households came together to cooperate on tasks like husking corn that were tedious for a single family, and entire neighborhoods turned out to clear timber or raise new houses and barns. At "huskings" in New England, men, women,

and children joined in the work, although only men took on the labor of hauling stones from fields at "stone bees," or spreading manure at "dunging frolics." Food, drink, and often dancing followed. Raisings were strenuous, even dangerous, but had a feel of contest and celebration. Large numbers of men and older boys came to erect the massive timber frames that the housewright had hewn and assembled on the ground. When the ridgepole was finally locked into place at the peak of the roof, the celebrations began. Men climbed up to perch atop the frame and drink a toast, and then "christened" the structure with a bottle of rum or a doggerel poem. Daring feats of balancing on the high cross-timbers or leaping from one to another often followed. Back on the ground, festive suppers were followed by wrestling competitions, and sometimes exuberant bouts of drinking.

The rhythms of social gatherings were primarily driven by the seasonal cycle of agricultural work. Winter was the quietest time of the farming year, when chores were lightest and days were short. But it was also a time when evening visits around the neighborhood became more frequent, as leisure time expanded and frozen roads often brought good traveling by sleigh. Neighbors gathered around the glowing hearth or sat at the table near the parlor stove to exchange old stories and sing ballads, to discuss last week's Sabbath sermon, to argue politics, or just to chat about other folk's affairs. Winter was also the busiest season for courting, when young people came together for parties, singing schools, sleigh rides, and dances. And, although stores did relatively light business in the

Raising the frame of the Fenno House Barn

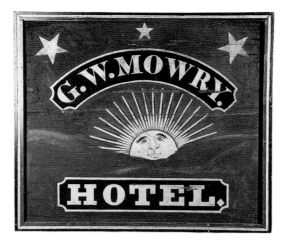

winter, they often stayed open into the evening as men assembled there to visit and catch up on the town's goings-on.

At all seasons of the year, a center village tavern on a busy road was likely to be crowded with stage drivers, teamsters, and travelers. Many men, villagers and farmers alike, came to the tavern to take a social glass, to hear the latest happenings, or to read a newspaper. Taproom walls were covered with handwritten notes about items for sale and town meeting warrants, as well as printed advertising broadsides and legal notices. New England taverns were usually more decorous than those in the West and South, but tavern life was sometimes rough and boisterous, and, on occasion, violent. There was a great deal of smoking and tobacco chewing, and frequently a good deal of drinking. Before 1820, most rural taverns had rooms for gambling—billiards, dice, and "playing at cards."

New England taverns increasingly welcomed women travelers as overnight guests, but their local clientele was almost exclusively male. By 1830 most taverns sought to achieve greater respectability by reserving one barroom for drovers, teamsters, stage drivers, and local tipplers, and a separate "parlor-barroom" for genteel travelers and more polished members of the community. Taverns were sometimes the scene for young people's sleighing parties, where they took a private room for punch and supper, music and storytelling, dancing and singing. Tavern ballrooms were often rented out for dances, as fiddles and flutes rang out late into the night at New Year's, Washington's Birthday, and election day.

By the 1830s, tavern life was changing. "Gaming," especially among prosperous and respectable men, was on the decline. America's first great temperance campaign, more successful in rural New England than anywhere else, was significantly diminishing the number of drinkers. In some communities, taverns closed to reopen as temperance hotels that sold no liquor. Most remained open, continued to sell rum and other "spirituous liquors," catered to expanding numbers of travelers, and became the preferred haunt of the "otherwise minded" who disliked ministers, deacons, and respectability.

Of the many places that make up the re-created historical landscape of Old Sturbridge Village, the Store, the District School, and the Meetinghouses speak most eloquently for the community. Such institutions drew the citizenry of country towns into the widening circles of public life. New Englanders opened their horizons to the greater world in these places: learned to read, traded widely with each other for goods from near and far, debated and voted on town affairs, listened to Scripture and innumerable sermons, and even discussed the morality of slavery. In such buildings, on the public space of the

Unloading goods at the Knight Store, as the storekeeper goes over the bill

common, and in their homes, they enacted the many occasions of community that bound them together—town meetings and election campaigns, Sabbath services and militia trainings, justice of the peace hearings and charitable society gatherings, lyceums and antislavery orations, agricultural fairs and Independence Day celebrations.

Asa Knight Store

Soon after Asa Knight opened for business in Dummerston, Vermont, some one hundred miles northwest of Sturbridge, in 1827, it became clear that his store was too small. Like hundreds of other rural merchants, he traded in produce from his country customers and offered for sale necessities and luxuries from New England, the United States, and the world. "Trade increases the wealth of a nation," Knight knew from his copy of the *Artist and Tradesman's Guide*, a popular storekeeper's manual, by bringing commodities "from places where they are plentiful, to those where they are scarce; and by providing a means for their more extended distribution." Knight linked his customers to far-flung markets for what they produced as well as to an expanding world of consumer goods. He built a

modest extension to the original single-story building, but by the 1830s, he needed much more space to stock the multiplying variety of commodities, imported and domestic, that had become available to "the country trade." Thus that structure was incorporated as an ell into the framing of a grand two-and-a-half-story emporium in 1838.

Products from most of the world's continents filled the display cases on the counter, crammed the drawers, were heaped up in boxes or barrels, and crowded the shelves in lustrous profusion clear up to the ceilings. Cloth was the most important single item on a country storekeeper's shelves, often amounting, as it did with Knight, to nearly half the value of his inventory. Most of these textiles were factory-produced—

New England country stores not only supplied their communities with a profusion of goods, but acted as centers for socializing and the exchange of information

Right: Partially unpacked goods in the Knight Store's office. English ceramics like those shown were shipped in open-work crates, packed in straw

printed calicoes and ginghams principally from England, plain cotton sheetings and shirtings from New England's own expanding mills, fine English woolens and American satinets. In smaller quantities there were cottons from France and India, central European and Irish linens, and even silks from Italy and China. The store was redolent with fragrances from far away: spices from the East Indies; sugar from the West Indies; tea from China; coffee from Arabia, Java, or Santo Domingo; currants from Greece; chocolate manufactured near Boston from South American cacao beans; Malaga wine; Holland gin; and West India rum.

English Staffordshire wares dominated the store's crockery shelves: "blue-edged" or "green-edged" plates and platters and transfer-printed dishes with views of exotic scenery. They were accompanied by colorfully banded mocha ware in smaller amounts and, for more utilitarian purposes, locally produced redware and New England–made stoneware. Hardware—latches, locks, screws, and nails—and cutlery were available from Birmingham in England. From New England's own fast-growing workshops came men's and women's shoes, farm implements and tools, window glass, stationery, schoolbooks and almanacs, tinware, brooms, baskets, and patent medicines.

Asa Knight and his fellow storekeepers would have acquired some of this profusion of goods from peddlers, commercial travelers, and local tradesmen, but for the great bulk of it they needed to turn to urban wholesalers and importers. Every year Knight took two extended buying trips to Boston, in the spring and fall. Staying in the city for a week each time, he visited a dozen or more wholesale merchants, inspected their seasonal offerings, settled previous accounts with cash from the sale of country produce, and bought goods to restock the store on six months' credit.

Very few of Knight's customers paid in cash. Instead, they provided him with goods that he could resell either in Boston, the major trading center for most New England country merchants, or closer to home. He principally sought butter and cheese, but in 1830 his daybook listed a remarkable medley of country produce—woolen hats and handwoven flannel, shoes and knitted socks, rye, corn, oats, ashes, beans, dried apples, and honey. Knight seems to have sold much of the butter, grain, and apples to customers nearby, but nearly every month he sent teamsters to Boston with loads of cheese. Chickens, geese, and turkeys were another country commodity that Knight sent to Boston. Each November he assembled flocks of poultry from Dummerston farms to be driven the 115 miles to Boston's Brighton market. Knight also found some profit in the palm-leaf hat trade in Dummerston, supplying materials to women working at home and shipping finished hats to Boston. For a few of the goods he took in, he was able to trade directly with nearby manufacturers: paying in handwoven flax tow cloth for window glass, buying books and paper in exchange for old rags, and exchanging beans for salt.

Country stores like Asa Knight's also served as community gathering places, information centers, and forums for public discussion and debate. Especially in the weeks right after harvest or just before spring planting, stores bustled with activity. Rows of horses and wagons or sleighs would be standing out front, while inside customers did their trading and conversed with their neighbors. Men talked crops and politics; women eagerly sought the latest news of births, marriages, and deaths. Every transaction at the store was a public event, carefully watched and overheard. The news—of towns and families offering unusual purchases and shrewd bargains—soon returned to homes in village and countryside.

Elizabeth Rollins of New Hampshire remembered her country store as "an unorganized lyceum" where center village folk and farmers gathered on many moonlit nights to hear wise and well-read tradesmen in active debate with the "college-learned lawyer and doctor." Conversations often grew jocular, except on those rare occasions when the minister dropped by. At different times—some followed an old New England tradition and preferred the week around New Year's—customers came to the store to settle their accounts. The merchant and his trading partners bent over the well-thumbed pages of the store ledger reconciling the "debtor to" and "credit by" entries. Balances were either paid or simply "brought forward" to begin the tally for a new year of trading. Stores became even more crowded when town meeting or election time approached, and local factions gathered to plot their strategies. Men came together to read the meeting warrant, to debate the merits of candidates, and to discuss how money should be spent on roads, schools, and the poor.

When Asa Knight died in 1851, his once-flourishing business was in decline, as rural Vermont began to lose population. After his eldest son, Randolph, finally closed the store forever in 1863, the main structure, with its original shelves, drawers, and counters, stood virtually unchanged in Dummerston until it was acquired almost a century later by Old Sturbridge Village. Detailed studies of the building revealed that the oldest part of the store, a small structure built in 1810, had been destroyed in 1909. When the building was moved to the museum and restored, this section was reconstructed using early photographs and archaeological evidence. The Knight Store differs strikingly from previous attempts to re-create early storekeeping. Its stock looks new. In order to portray the store as it would have looked to its customers in the late 1830s, the museum undertook extensive research both on country store merchandise and on the packaging and labeling of goods in the period. Original artifacts were combined with hundreds of carefully reproduced items of stock—plus barrels, crates, boxes, papers, packages, and labels—to give the store the bright look of an active "center of commerce."

District School

"The principal allurement and prime happiness of going to school as it used to be conducted," claimed Warren Burton in his classic 1835 account of *The District School As It Was,* "was the opportunity it afforded for social amusement." For children who lived on outlying farms scattered a half-mile or quarter-mile apart, brothers and sisters were often their only playmates, and going to school was their first significant contact with other children in the community. For older children, seeing their friends every day made the winter school term seem like a series of "holydays" compared to the spring, summer, and fall months when they were kept busy helping their families in kitchens or fields. "Many of the children would not see each other between schools," remembered a blacksmith's daughter from rural New Hampshire, "which was only three months in the summer and the same in the winter."

Students of all ages and both sexes went to school in the winter term, while ordinarily only younger children attended during the summer when farm and household work pressed the older ones. Attendance was not compulsory, but all the New England states except Rhode Island had, since long before the Revolution, required towns to provide tax-supported schooling for all children. By the 1830s the great majority of New England towns were divided into between six and fifteen neighborhood districts with a school in each, and virtually every household was within walking distance of a schoolhouse. As

a result, the level of basic literacy among rural New Englanders was strikingly high. Some 90 percent or more of the population could read, "cipher," or do basic arithmetic, and write—although their spelling might often strike us as inventive.

District schools were one-room structures that housed as few as twenty or as many as seventy children during a five-and-a-half-day school week, usually from nine to three o'clock. Children as young as two were sometimes sent to school, following along with older brothers and sisters, although four was a more common age to begin. Schooling could continue through the teens, as young people whose early attendance had been sporadic strove to complete their education. At times, "big boys and girls" of seventeen and eighteen shared the ungraded classroom with pupils whom we today would consider preschoolers.

Schools did not provide texts, and parents supplied their children with a wide variety of books, both new and out-of-date, so teachers made individual assignments and heard recitations when the students were ready. Four-year-olds started a spelling book, very often Noah Webster's famous "Blue-Back Speller" with its 150 lessons, and began their first reading lessons. At about seven or eight, students were introduced to geography, using books that challenged them to memorize lengthy selections of facts about the population, cities, products, and chief characteristics of New England, the United States, South America, and the rest of the world. Penmanship was introduced to students at nine or so, after they had mastered the use of slates and slate pencils. Arithmetic was taken up between ages ten and twelve, along with more difficult reading assign-

Two students recite at the teacher's desk in the District School, while the others concentrate on their lessons

Opposite: The District School

ments. District school readers were usually formidable anthologies of English and American essays, orations, sermons, and poetry. The Bible was occasionally used as a reader, but direct religious instruction was very rare, reserved instead for home, Sunday meeting, and Sabbath School. Some older students took up American history as texts appeared in the 1830s, while fewer studied European history. Grammar texts were dry and difficult collections of rules to be memorized, and little attention was paid to improving speech or writing style.

Since school attendance varied so much from one family to another, some students completed the entire curriculum while others received only a smattering of knowledge. Repetition, memorization, and recitation were the hallmarks of district school instruction. When students assigned to study the same subject were ready to be tested, they were called to the "recitation benches" near the teacher's desk. Then, with bows and curtsies, they answered set questions in reading, grammar, arithmetic, or geography. Good pedagogy called for them to be quizzed one by one, but often, to save time, a teacher would simply ask the entire group to recite their lessons in unison. With this stress on rote learning, New Englanders often enough recalled "getting by heart" long lists of grammatical rules or entire essays that they never fully understood.

Teachers (an earlier term, still in use, was schoolmaster) were young and unmarried, rarely more than twenty-five and occasionally no older than seventeen. Young men went into teaching as a way station to something else, sometimes to earn money to continue their college education. There were no formal qualifications for teachers, who were

usually hired, sometimes after an oral examination, by town committees. As part of their compensation they "boarded around" the district, staying a week each with a number of local families.

Crowding, a bewilderingly wide range of ages and capacities, and the teachers' own youth often made discipline hard to maintain. Schoolmasters sought to increase the distance between themselves and their pupils with formality in dress and rituals of curt-sying and bowing by the students. Many, perhaps most, relied on punishment as well, ranging from inflicting relatively mild embarrassment to severe whipping. On occasion, a young teacher had to prove himself in physical combat against the school's "big boys" or find himself "barred out" from the school and his employment ignominiously ended.

Traditionally, women had been hired to teach only in the summer term, and then only the youngest children. Older pupils, it was thought, needed a man's firm hand. But by the 1830s this was changing. Even country school committees were increasingly see-ing women as more effective teachers than men for elementary subjects. They could keep order with "moral suasion" instead of corporal punishment, avoid confrontations and "barring out"—and be paid less in the bargain. They began to teach in the winter term as well.

This view of Miss Gorham's Seminary was probably painted by a student. Hundreds of small private schools in New England provided young men and women with education beyond district schooling (Anonymous watercolor, c. 1820–30)

The District School at Old Sturbridge Village, built between 1800 and 1810 in Candia, New Hampshire, about seventy-five miles northeast of Sturbridge, is a stark building with a narrow vestibule and a single schoolroom. Without clapboarding, it stands simply in its sheathing boards. Situated on an otherwise useless corner of land with no space for a playground, it shows few external signs recognizable today of being a place for teaching children. On a gently sloping floor, rows of battered scholars' desks face the teacher's tall desk near the simple box stove and a couple of old chairs for guests. The stove heats the schoolroom better than a fireplace would have, but the room is still bare and dimly lit. There are no maps, globes, or blackboards, for these were notions of improvement whose worth most rural district taxpayers would still have questioned.

Schools were often the only public buildings in their neighborhoods and served as informal centers of community in the evening or when classes were not in session. School district meetings, miniature versions of the town meeting that brought a couple of dozen neighborhood taxpayers together, were held here, as were the occasional inter-views with prospective teachers. People came to the schoolhouse for evening spelling competitions, singing schools, revival meetings, and sometimes even antislavery lectures.

New England's schools were better than those anywhere else in the United States, but by the 1830s they were being subjected to rigorous scrutiny by a new and vigorous movement for educational reform. The traditional district school system had produced several generations of reasonably literate men and women, but the reformers were concerned with its deficiencies, not its achievements. A changing New England in a changing nation, they argued, needed to provide an education that better prepared its citizens for their responsibilities. They wanted to standardize textbooks, reduce or elim-inate corporal punishment and barring out, keep the very youngest children at home, and ensure that the "big boys and girls" finished their elementary schooling earlier. In addi-tion, they had two other dramatic innovations in mind: the development of institutions that would actually train teachers and the physical reshaping of the schoolhouse itself. Unlike traditional rural schoolhouses, virtually all of which resembled the Candia school, new improved school buildings were to have better lighting and ventilation, blackboards, globes, maps, single-seat desks, and fenced-in schoolyards. Newly trained teachers would emphasize comprehension rather than rote memorization and guide stu-dents toward an understanding of principles as well as facts.

The leading spokesmen for educational reform—men like Horace Mann of Massachusetts and Henry Barnard of Connecticut—achieved enduring reputations, but were deeply frustrated by the uneven, halting pace of change. Some rural New Englanders embraced the cause, proposing new schoolhouse designs, the hiring of better-qualified teachers, and even the raising of taxes to pay for them. Many others resisted for years. In the late 1830s there were some signs of change. There were fewer very young or very big students, more women teachers, and less corporal punishment. In many cen-ter villages, prosperous and progressive citizens voted for the building of improved, bet-ter-equipped schools. In most of the countryside, however, the old-fashioned district school would remain much as it was for another decade or two.

Opportunities for education beyond the district school were still for the few, not the many. There were a very few tax-supported "high" or "grammar" schools in large communities, but most secondary education was provided by private academies that could be found in every county seat and in a significant scattering of other towns. In the 1830s academy attendance was growing, and perhaps one student in ten went on to take at least a term or two of secondary learning. Academies for men provided some instruction in foreign languages, advanced English composition, mathematics, natural science, history, and geography. Those for women had earlier focused largely on training in various forms of music, painting, drawing, embroidery, and other domestic accomplishments, but were increasingly offering academic courses as well and seeking to prepare some of their pupils for teaching. Finally, New England could boast a dozen men's colleges in the 1830s (collegiate education for women was not yet a reality), but only a very small minority of rural New Englanders could afford or aspire to higher learning. It was rare enough that through the nineteenth century virtually all the published histories of rural towns proudly included the short lists of their college graduates.

Center Meetinghouse

The graceful white meetinghouse on the town common, both a house of worship and a center for public assembly, had by the 1830s already become the defining image of the rural New England town. Religious societies founded in the seventeenth or eighteenth century generally maintained their dominant presence in the early nineteenth, either remodeling an inherited building or raising the heavy frame of a new structure. In most center villages there would be two or three meetinghouses, but sometimes only one, usually the Congregational, fronted on the town common. Collective expressions of a commitment to moral and spiritual order, they were usually built in as elegant a form as parishioners could afford. The stately example now overlooking the Common at the Village was built in 1832, when the fashionable simplicity of the Greek Revival style was sweeping across New England. With its bright white paint and Paris green shutters and doors, it dominates its surroundings. The strength of its simple design lies in its bold symmetrical forms: angular moldings and cornices, widely spaced columns, and a towering belfry and steeple.

The Center Meetinghouse at Old Sturbridge Village stood originally in the center village of the town of Sturbridge itself, where it was erected by the Baptist Society in 1832. A few years later, in 1838, it was moved two miles to the nearby manufacturing village of Fiskdale, as the town's population center changed. Early-nineteenth-century buildings were moved with surprising frequency, jacked up off their foundations onto heavy carriage frames and hauled to their new locations by multiple teams of oxen. The Meetinghouse, like other large buildings, was cut in two for the move and then rejoined. Well over a hundred years later the Meetinghouse was moved again. Its Baptist congregation wished to join with another denomination and move to its church building; Old Sturbridge Village acquired the structure in exchange for providing the now joined congregations with a new organ. For its move to the museum, the building was carefully dismantled and reassembled.

Opposite: The Center Meetinghouse

The Congregationalists—direct heirs of the Puritans—remained New England's largest Protestant denomination and were dominant in many communities. New England's Baptists had branched off from Congregationalism during the religious ferment of the First Great Awakening in the 1740s; their beliefs differed in some crucial aspects but the two denominations were broadly similar in practice and organization. In the years after 1800, Unitarians were growing in number as they separated, often with painful conflict, from "orthodox" Congregationalists; they were heavily concentrated in eastern Massachusetts. Through much of the countryside there was a scattering of Universalists, with their distinctive belief in the salvation of all mankind, and of Friends, with their even more distinctive testimonies of pacifism and plainness of speech and dress. In Connecticut, Episcopalians flourished in a number of country towns. By the 1830s the Methodists were New England's fastest-growing denomination, building their chapels in factory villages and outlying neighborhoods. Catholics had previously been very few, but the region's growing number of Irish immigrants were beginning to build city churches; those few who had come to live in the country awaited itinerant priests to celebrate Mass in private homes. Jews were still a tiny minority with only one formally organized synagogue in Newport, Rhode Island.

In the Puritan tradition, the meetinghouse had never been called a "church," since that word properly referred only to the select body of "visible saints" themselves, who testified to their conversion or "new birth" and signed the covenant. In addition to the members of "the Church," however, a substantially larger group of men and women, "the

Society," supported the minister, maintained the meetinghouse, and attended worship. Except in Rhode Island, Congregationalism had been New England's de facto "established church" before the Revolution, with the town, and the religious society that extended over the same territory, considered virtually identical. Traditionally then, Congregational meetinghouses were used for town meetings and elections as well as for religious worship. And the practice of using local taxes to support religious worship remained longer here than anywhere else in the United States.

Connecticut and Massachusetts did not completely dismantle their old systems of compulsory religious taxation until 1818 and, finally, 1833, respectively. The dual use of the meetinghouse lingered for decades. Although some larger communities began to build separate town halls, center village meetinghouses—usually Congregationalist or Unitarian, but sometimes Baptist or Universalist—continued to serve as the primary sites for town meetings, concerts, lectures, and celebrations—as well as for Sunday worship services—throughout the 1830s.

New England theology had a long and highly complicated evolution in the over two hundred years from the Pilgrims' initial settlement to the 1830s. There was substantial diversity of belief and sometimes still fierce disputation. For Congregationalists and Baptists, some of the Calvinistic harshness of Puritanism had softened on points like predestination and infant damnation. Almost all New England Protestants now agreed that both human effort and God's grace had a role to play in salvation; for most Methodists, Baptists, and Congregationalists, the crucial way to seek God's kingdom was through "revivals of religion"—intense waves of enthusiasm that washed over communities and brought newly converted members into the churches. The revivals of the Second Great Awakening had begun in New England in the 1790s, and had fluctuated but never disappeared in following decades. In hundreds of rural communities the 1830s were a time of great evangelical fervor.

Not everyone in New England went to meeting every Sunday, but the Puritan tradition of strict observance of the Sabbath remained strong. Travel on the Sabbath, except to attend meeting, was discouraged, although no longer banned outright. All taverns, stores, shops, and mills were expected to remain closed. Work in the fields ceased, and in many households even cooking chores were customarily suspended. Most households attended worship services somewhat regularly, and for many families it was the crucial event of the week. Congregational worship services (and those of most other Protestant denominations) were two to three hours long, both in the morning and the afternoon. Psalms, hymns, extemporaneous prayers, anthems by the "singers," and lengthy Scripture readings were arranged around the minister's morning and afternoon sermons. Each sermon was carefully written out, meticulously supplied with biblical references, and never less than an hour in length. They tended to focus on important theological and scriptural issues, but sometimes there was "near preaching"—a sermon addressed to a specific problem or group of individuals in the community. Interest ran high, even though drowsy heads might occasionally nod; a great many sermons were printed by request and much discussed. During the break between services, members of the congregation adjourned for their cold noon meals, cooked the day before. Some joined friends who lived close by or went to the parsonage, while many simply ate in their pews or in wagons and carriages. In better weather they might take their meals outdoors on the grass.

Although toddlers, infants, and nursing mothers did not usually come to meeting, older children ordinarily attended with their parents and, by the 1830s, sat together in the family pew. As some New Englanders remembered their childhood, going to meeting was a difficult ordeal. In the most pious families, play, nonreligious conversation and reading, even laughter, were often forbidden throughout the day. For the devout, the Sabbath remained a day of blessed quiet and spiritual satisfaction. Still others saw the weekly ritual as a welcome diversion, for sober as the services were, Sunday as a whole was a pivotal social event for many families. New England's center villages bustled in the morning when people from the surrounding countryside streamed in for worship. Rows of unhitched carriages and wagons stood near the long horse sheds beside the meetinghouse, and meeting-goers' mounts occupied every available hitching spot in the village. Families renewed their ties with the friends and kin they seldom saw during the week and exchanged news. Men and women took the occasion to display their finest clothes, and young people especially hoped for some brief chance to socialize before and between the services.

Sabbath day services are periodically re-created at the Center Meetinghouse so that museum visitors can experience the distinctive character of public worship in early New England. Much as a visitor to a New England meetinghouse found in 1839, "the minister speaks from a mahogany desk; he reposes his hands upon its covering of scarlet velvet." The services are far shorter than they would have been then, but they include early-nineteenth-century hymns and anthems performed by the singers, prayers and Scripture readings, and powerful excerpts from sermons that were first delivered in the 1830s.

This meetinghouse of the 1830s is not as physically austere as its eighteenth-century predecessor would have been. Its crimson pulpit drapery, mahogany pulpit and communion table, and "Grecian" sofa and parlor chairs are up-to-date echoes of the genteel furnishings of prosperous homes. A more traditional note is struck by the old-fashioned box pews, made of plain pine but painted and "grained" to resemble oak. In the early nineteenth century each pew would have belonged to a family; their auctioning and sale, and yearly "pew rent" paid to the society, was the primary financial support of many churches, particularly after religious taxation ended. The cost of pews depended on the prestige of their location, those in the center and closest to the pulpit having the highest value. Their owners personalized them, and made themselves comfortable with carpeting, seat cushions, footstools, and armrests—creating a colorful hodgepodge as seen from the galleries above.

The organ standing to the right of the pulpit is also a sign of change. Singing in early Puritan meetinghouses had been unaccompanied. Gradually, with much debate and dissension, bass viols (similar to modern cellos) and occasionally other instruments came into use to accompany the singers. A couple of generations later, in the early nineteenth century, pipe organs were introduced into country meetinghouses to support choral and congregational singing. This proved controversial as well, reminding some parishioners too much of Catholic and Episcopal worship. By 1840 organs, as signs of affluence and

Opposite: The Friends' Meetinghouse

musical sophistication, were generally although not universally accepted.

Traditionally, all gatherings at the meetinghouse took place in daylight hours. In winter, afternoon services were started an hour earlier so farm families could reach home by twilight. However, under the impetus of the revivals of the Second Great Awakening, many religious societies began to hold additional meetings on Sunday nights and weekday evenings. A wooden chandelier, with shiny tin reflectors and twelve candle cups, reproduced from a rare original, hangs from the center of the ceiling of the Village's Center Meetinghouse. Such items, as the Reverend William Bentley said in 1810, had once been "a rare thing in our churches," and reflect the increasing nighttime use of the buildings.

Since meetinghouses had never been considered "sacred" spaces in the Puritan tradition, there was often a striking informality in the ways New Englanders used them, even during services on the Sabbath. Singers in the gallery might perform with distractingly flamboyant gestures, and some worshipers chewed tobacco and spit in the aisles. When the door was open in summer, turkeys or geese were likely to wander in, and dogs often followed their masters into the meetinghouse. At least one minister went on record to chide his hearers for noisily chewing nuts and fruits in their pews and strewing the refuse on the floor. Beginning in the 1820s, a younger generation of ministers and their more genteel parishioners were making concerted efforts to "improve" the decorum of worship. They banned dogs, shamed tobacco chewers, and discouraged snacking during services.

On public occasions—town meetings, elections, Fourth of July celebrations, lyceums—meetinghouses became civic spaces again. During town meeting, the decorous behavior that ministers and congregations had struggled to achieve usually disappeared. Voters sat wherever they wished in the pews; pew owners suspended their rights when the structures were used for secular gatherings and simply hoped their fellow townsmen would be careful of the furnishings. Men rose to speak, milled about, and during elections crowded around the clerk's table and ballot box. Concerts, lectures, and public orations brought more "refined" audiences. Political, economic, and religious change was altering the texture of rural life, but the meetinghouse persisted at the New England community's center.

Friends' Meetinghouse

Members of the Society of Friends, or Quakers, were not a conspicuous presence everywhere in New England in the 1830s, but they were significant beyond their numbers. On Sunday mornings in one town out of twelve—while hundreds of smartly attired worshipers were gathering for services to the pealing of bells—a small group of modestly dressed Quakers would be filing into the stillness of their plain, undecorated meetinghouse. Holding firmly to their belief that salvation came only as a direct experience of the "light within," the Friends had no use or regard for soaring steeples, learned ministers,

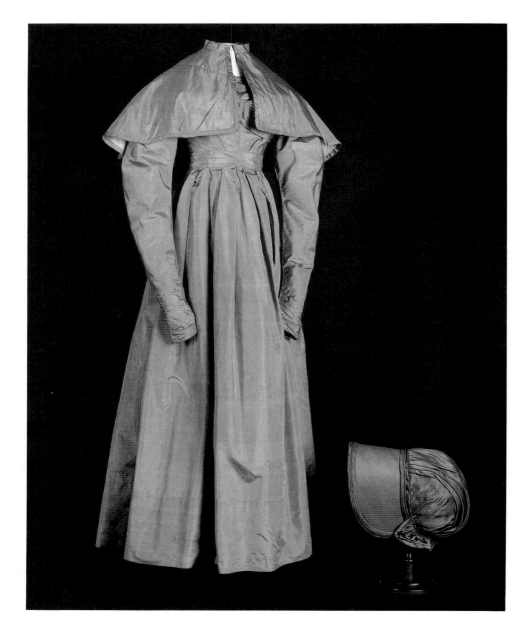

This silk dress and bonnet c. 1830 were first owned by Chloe Gifford, who belonged to a Friends' Meeting in West Falmouth, Massachusetts. They are up-to-date in cut, but unornamented and sedate in color

elaborate theologies, or the trappings of ritual. Even the Sabbath itself was simply "First Day" to the Friends, who rejected the traditional names of days and months as pagan in origin.

Called Quakers since the mid-seventeenth century, when their English founder, George Fox, had bidden them to "Tremble at the word of the Lord," the Friends had kept on a determined, and different, course. Based on their understanding of Scripture and God's revealed will, they refused to bear arms or take oaths and were uncompromisingly "plain" in dress, speech, and manners. Persecuted in the seventeenth century for their radical beliefs, New England's Quakers eventually earned a grudging tolerance and then acceptance in the eighteenth. Even in the nineteenth century, they continued to cluster in their small communities and remained a people apart. Overall, their numbers constituted less than 1 percent of the region's population; some ninety of the Friends' conspicuously stark meetinghouses were scattered throughout the New England states.

In the small state of Rhode Island, notable for religious toleration from the earliest days
of colonization, there were Friends' meetings in over half the towns in 1830. Elsewhere,
Friends were fewest in Connecticut, Vermont, and New Hampshire, more likely to be
found in Maine and Massachusetts.

The Friends' Meetinghouse at the Village was built in 1796 in Bolton, about
thirty miles northeast of Sturbridge and one of the seven rural towns in central
Massachusetts's Worcester County that had such meetings. Some of these meetinghouses
stood near center villages, but most, like the one in Bolton, were located in an outlying
area and surrounded by a small Quaker community. The space around the Meetinghouse,
unlike the structures of other denominations, is marked off by stone walls and gates, evidence in the landscape of the Friends' "separation from the world." Without a steeple,
large windows, or imposing entrance, the structure is painted dove-gray with white
trim. The small entryway opens into a space with whitewashed walls, barren of all orna-
ment. There is no altar, pulpit, or communion table. On "First Day," and again in mid-
week, whole families came to worship, sitting separated by gender on plain wooden
benches. No minister read Scripture or preached, although the meeting's elders, both men
and women, usually sat on benches at the front that faced the congregation. They met in
silent prayer until one and then another might be moved by the Spirit to pray aloud or
speak his or her concerns. No one—man or woman—was forbidden to speak, and yet
some meetings could pass entirely in silence.

Opposed to professional clergymen, whom they called a "hireling ministry," the
Friends ministered to one another and interpreted Scripture for themselves. They were
guided in worship, principles of propriety, and administration by laypeople of both

sexes, who were chosen as elders. During monthly meetings to discuss business, partitions were lowered to divide men and women, expressly to enhance equality. Decisions required the consent of both groups, but before they were discussed by all together, the women had an opportunity to speak among themselves without the intimidating presence of fathers and husbands. In New England and elsewhere, Quakers firmly believed in the equality of all people under God. Some Friends, impelled by their convictions, were among America's earliest and most powerful advocates for the abolition of slavery and for other measures of social reform. Most Friends lived quietly and separately, keeping "clear of the world."

Social Occasions Re-created

"They have few holidays," complained Englishwoman Margaret Hall while traveling in New England in 1828–29. Compared to Old England, the New England calendar did seem remarkably sparse. In the view of the Puritan founders, none of the old holidays of the Church of England were ever sanctioned by Scripture, and so they were abolished. Christmas and Easter were swept away with other rituals and festivities, and those days remained uncelebrated and largely unnoticed by most New Englanders well into the nineteenth century. Gradually a distinctive New England calendar emerged, and the holidays and other occasions for celebration or remembrance that were observed in the region in the 1830s are re-created in the Village today.

Thanksgiving

Long before it became an American national holiday, Thanksgiving was the great and distinctive religious festival of New England. It originated with special days of celebration that were proclaimed by Puritan magistrates to rejoice in good harvests, deliverance from disease, or other instances of divine favor. It gradually became a yearly harvest observance in the late seventeenth century, and the most important ritual of New England life for many decades thereafter. Proclaimed each year in late November or early December by the governors of each state, the "day of public thanksgiving and praise" traditionally commenced with a meetinghouse service in the morning, which was followed by family feasting in virtually every home throughout the rest of the day.

During the last week in November, kitchens at the Village are bustling as they were 160 years ago with preparations for the great day. Shelves are piled high with sauces, pickles, and preserves; the air is filled with aromas of breads and pies baking in the ovens, and a charity basket is being packed for the poor—all reminding visitors of the historical links between Thanksgivings past and present. Sometime during the week,

Thanksgiving dinner at the Freeman Farmhouse

men assemble with smoothbore muskets and rifles for a turkey shoot, to see who can win the prize in an early-nineteenth-century target competition. On the long-anticipated day itself, interpreters in Village households crowd around laden tables for the great feast's traditional fare of roast turkey and chicken pies; sweet butter and honey, breads and steaming gravies; boiled squash, turnips, onions, and potatoes; mincemeats, plum puddings, and cranberry sauce; pumpkin, apple, and Marlborough pies. For visitors, the historical Thanksgiving festivities are a prelude to their own celebrations. Many have returned to the Village on Thanksgiving Day for a decade or more.

Weddings and Funerals

Public celebration and mourning marked the community's observance of two rites of passage: marriage and death. Periodically, Old Sturbridge Village finds ways to share the historical re-creation of these most public of private events.

Weddings were traditionally performed at home, and the week around Thanksgiving was a favorite "marrying time" for Yankee brides. In the 1830s, weddings were much quieter affairs than they had been at the beginning of the century. Whereas

it had once been customary to invite the entire neighborhood to a celebration of dining and dancing after the ceremony, some New England couples now were seeking smaller, more genteel, weddings—sometimes limited only to their closest kin and a few friends.

Rarely in New England had the wedding ceremony itself been long or elaborate; in the best parlor of the bride's home, a black-clad clergyman stood before the couple, their "groomsmen" and bridesmaids, and led them through a brief exchange of vows without music, procession, or ritual trappings. Some 1830s weddings were downright sedate and "temperate," without wine for toasting the new couple's health or dancing to celebrate. Others held on to as much of the traditional merrymaking as they respectably could. A sizable and elaborate wedding cake, days in preparation, was still part of the ceremony.

Brides wore their best dresses, more likely to be dove-gray or brown than white, and grooms wore formal black. Presents were uncommon, but couples were beginning to take "nuptial journeys"—often a week or two to visit relatives, occasionally a lengthier trip, even to "the Falls of Niagara"! When a wedding is re-created at the Village, the

Above: With the Fenno House's mirrors and pictures covered to express sorrow, a pine coffin strewn with herbs awaits the arrival of other mourners in the village's re-creation of a funeral service

Opposite: A characteristically simple marriage ceremony of the 1830s re-created in the Salem Towne House parlor

simple ceremony is surrounded by the scurry and excitement of preparations in the households. The "bride" and "groom" can be encountered during the day as they await the ceremony, the wedding cake is in preparation, and the community is full of conversation and gossip.

By the standards of its time, rural New England was a healthy place, but death—whether from sickness, old age, or accident—was in the early nineteenth century still a common visitor that families encountered at home. Its rituals were austere and, of necessity, carried out without delay. News of each death spread quickly through small communities, and the meetinghouse bell was soon tolling in a pattern that rang out the status—usually five strokes for a child, seven for a woman, and nine for a man—and then the age of the deceased. Neighbors came to help family members "lay out" and wash the corpse at home, and quickly cut and sew the shroud. The coffin, hastily commissioned from a nearby carpenter, would lie open in the best room. Mourners assembled to await the minister, who would pray, sometimes preach, and then lead the procession to the graveyard.

As late as the first decade of the nineteenth century, crowds of mourners came back to the house for abundant funeral feasts and sometimes excessive quantities of strong drink. When the Village re-creates a funeral, however, it depicts the newer custom of the 1830s, when funeral sermons were more often given at the meetinghouse and funeral "entertainments" were more sober and private. Interpreters portraying mourners, some dressed wholly in black and others with crepe armbands and ribbons, gather first at the home of the grieving family. All—including visitors—then join in the somber funeral procession and attend the service at the Center Meetinghouse. Afterward, kinfolk and neighbors return to the house for a post-funeral meal.

Singing and Dancing

Music and dance were enormously important in an age without mass media, and, at various times and places, they touched the lives of almost every New Englander. Around the kitchen fireside, in the parlor, at the meetinghouse, in shops, fields, or taverns, New Englanders came together to sing. Traditional English and Scottish ballads had come with the first settlers, and new ones arose recounting remarkable events in the New World. These most traditional of songs were rarely written down, and they expanded into numerous variations as they were passed along from singer to singer over the generations. Country folk also sang words from printed broadsides or small books called "songsters" to well-known tunes. At least a few of these songs were profane, most likely heard only at taverns or boisterous men's working parties. However, in many New England households, secular songs gave way to religious music. Many hymns and psalm tunes first learned at the meetinghouse became "popular" music, sung virtually everywhere.

Every winter all over New England, country schoolhouses and, sometimes, meetinghouses would resonate to the "joyful noise" of singing schools. They offered

evening lessons to groups of subscribers who hoped to learn enough to deliver a respectable performance in public worship. "Singing masters" generally traveled from town to town, seeking employment training choirs in the rudiments of reading music and four-part singing. The singers practiced, sometimes two or three times a week, until they had completed twenty or thirty lessons; then they often gave a "singing exhibition."

The songs and instrumental melodies of the countryside are still performed at Old Sturbridge Village. A singing school may meet to prepare hymns and anthems for Sunday services. Men play the fiddle or flute, instruments traditional in the country; women sing unaccompanied or play sentimental songs and rousing marches on the Towne House parlor's pianoforte. A fife-and-drum detachment regularly performs New England's "martial music." Old ballads may occasionally be heard, and even such humble instruments as bones, spoons, and mouth harps are part of a lively informal repertoire.

"The dancing was in my very feet," remembered a woman about her girlhood in the 1830s, "the violin haunted me." Dancing was a widely popular entertainment among New Englanders of all sorts, from farmers' daughters and shoe peggers to lawyers and ladies of fashion. There was a plentiful variety of occasions—from impromptu gatherings, huskings, and raisings, to sleighing parties and balls. Just as today, no one danced more often than young people of courting age, and their diaries frequently mention danc-

An impromptu dance on the floor of the Freeman Barn

ing parties that lasted until three or four in the morning. "There were thirty-five couples. We staid until about day," wrote Pamela Brown of an 1836 ball in Plymouth, Vermont, where she had danced until she was "about tired of it."

Although dancing had long been a widely accepted part of community life, it was coming under widespread criticism through the first decades of the nineteenth century. During the revivals of the 1830s, many, perhaps most, of New England's clergy were setting their faces against it. To them, it was a worldly indulgence, stressing the body at the expense of the spirit, and they succeeded in convincing a significant number of their parishioners to stop. Observers at the time agreed that the number of dancers in most communities fell when a religious revival was at its peak and rose again after fervor had declined. But many New Englanders, certainly most young men and women, continued to dance.

Some were alarmed by the intimacy of the newest dance fashion of the 1830s, the "valse," in which couples danced alone—closely facing one another. But the waltz was only occasionally seen in the countryside. The traditional dances of New England were English reels and contradances that arranged men and women in two long, facing lines and sent them chasing up and down the lines in pairs through a sequence of whirling steps. Everyone still knew these steps in the early nineteenth century, but the younger generation was widely adopting the cotillion or quadrille, a French style that took the country dance figures and rearranged them for four couples.

Fiddles, and sometimes flutes, provided dance music, and whenever Village interpreters gather for a dance on special days on the museum's calendar, there is a fiddler to set the couples in motion. Village dancers perform on most of the occasions when their early New England predecessors would have danced—Independence Day, militia trainings, harvest celebrations, and other "occasions to meet together." They are sometimes formal, with dancers in their best attire accompanied by several musicians, and sometimes impromptu, with a single fiddler playing for a handful of revelers taking time from their work.

Storytelling

New Englanders of the 1830s had access to books, weekly newspapers, and some monthly magazines, and read more than previous generations had done; but information traveled slowly and there was still room in their lives for stories. By the kitchen fireside or the shop stove, stories filled many a winter evening, and accomplished storytellers were always appreciated. Anecdotes of family and local history, tales of youthful adventures, or preposterous yarns and instructive fables were recounted to each new generation. There were supernatural tales of apparitions and suspected witchcraft; reminiscences of the hardships of settlement; stories of travel to Boston, New York, or the West; and narratives of the Revolutionary War and the War of 1812. Only rarely written down, these stories were passed along from teller to listener during family gatherings and neighborly visits, or at tavern soirees and evenings at the store. Stories entertained and passed the time, but they also connected people to each other and passed on beliefs, personal histories, and shared experiences. At the Village today, the storytelling tradition of rural New England continues. In a cozy chimney corner, out under the shade of an apple tree, at a gathering near the Fenno House barn, or in the museum's formal Brick Theatre, interpreters engage visitors in the oral traditions of an almost vanished past.

Town Meeting

Held at least once each year in every one of New England's more than a thousand towns, the town meeting, in the words of nineteenth-century America's most perceptive foreign observer, Alexis de Tocqueville, brought "liberty within the people's reach." Today, it is still considered a vital model of democratic decision making. The meeting day, fixed by statute, was in March in most states, signaling the beginning of the civil as well as the agricultural year. The term of winter schooling often began the day after Thanksgiving and ended the day before the March meeting.

In the 1830s, town meetings in all the New England states but Rhode Island—where heavy property and inheritance qualifications still prevailed—gave the substantial majority of men over twenty-one a chance to debate and vote on the affairs of the community. Rhode Island and Connecticut restricted voting to whites; elsewhere it was open to men regardless of race. These restrictions were real, but nowhere else in the world at that time was political power so widely shared.

Town meeting procedure was governed by dry official guides such as Isaac Goodwin's *Town Officer*, but the reality was often noisy and outspoken, sometimes humorous, and sometimes tense and conflict-ridden. For its re-created town meetings, Old Sturbridge Village has drawn upon the detailed minutes kept by town clerks six generations ago, testimony in judicial cases involving town affairs, and the reminiscences of many participants.

Two weeks in advance of the meeting, several copies of the warrant, or agenda, were made up by the selectmen (elected officials who governed the town under the meeting's direction) and posted in public places around town—at meetinghouses, taverns, and stores. A long list of town officers had to be elected and action was required on taxation and expenditures—raising and allocating money for state and county expenses and for the town's roads, schools, and poor relief. Selectmen, clerk, treasurer, tax assessors and collectors, school committees, and highway supervisors had to be chosen yearly. Fence viewers were elected to arbitrate disputes over boundaries, and a pound keeper was required to pen up straying animals—cattle, horses, sheep, or hogs—in a secure town enclosure until they were claimed by the owners. "Hogreeves" were no longer much needed to round up wandering pigs who might damage fields and gardens, but the office was usually filled as a joke. Each year, it was a customary gesture for all men newly married since the last meeting to be elected hogreeve. When their times came, Pliny

Freeman, Emerson Bixby, and Salem Towne, Jr., all held the obligatory office.

Roads and schools often preoccupied the town meeting—as they continue to do in small-town America. The meeting laid out new roads, occasionally abandoned unused ones, but was primarily concerned with the pick-and-shovel, oxcart, and stone-drag work of maintaining them. The "highway tax" could be required to be paid in labor on the roads rather than in cash to pay hired workers. Individual school districts taxed themselves to build and maintain schoolhouses, but the appropriation for teachers' salaries was voted by the town meeting as a whole.

The care of the poor—"paupers" who were without resources and had no kin to care for them—was a local responsibility. Most town paupers were chronically ill, disabled, elderly, or very young orphans. Towns confirmed by vote each year the manner in which they should be assisted. "Outdoor relief," or deliveries of firewood and food supplies, was commonly arranged for the needy who had their own homes. For the poor who needed lodging and even medical care, as well as food and clothing, the "vendue" system was widely in use. It was an auction that, at the directions of the Overseers of the Poor, placed paupers completely in the care of the lowest bidders, who were paid from the town treasury. During the 1820s, many New Englanders came to think of the vendue as demeaning to the poor and susceptible of abuse. They sought new approaches to poor relief. Often, they resolved, as did the town of Sturbridge in 1829, to refuse vendue bids from "any person that is not a responsible man as to character and property." Many communities began to consider purchasing a farm to lodge the poor and provide them some self-supporting work. Town farms, run by a superintending farmer and his family, were widely adopted by town vote, as both more humane and, hopefully, less expensive in the long run. After struggling with proposals and committees of enquiry for five years, Sturbridge eventually decided in 1835 to move its seventeen town citizens then on poor relief to a suitably equipped 117-acre farm.

Washington's Birthday

George Washington's birthday was celebrated even while the great general was alive. His death in 1799 brought a display of public sentiment unprecedented in New England, as virtually all the region's clergymen preached funeral sermons in his honor and hundreds of towns organized solemn memorial processions. Within a few years, the first president had been immortalized as the chief symbol of American nationality. Into the 1830s, many New Englanders continued to revere his memory and to celebrate the day with elaborate balls and ceremonious orations. At Old Sturbridge Village, Washington's Birthday returns to life as a real holiday every February, with a special Meetinghouse service of celebration, music and toasts to "the grand Apostle of Liberty," and the telling of grandfathers' stories about the Revolutionary War.

Independence Day

The Fourth of July was New England's—and the new republic's—most exuberant holiday, a virtually universal celebration of national identity. Beginning in 1776, when the Declaration of Independence was read to the assembled citizens of Boston, the holiday ritual quickly took its distinctive shape—martial music and military exercises on the common, a procession of citizens and a celebratory feast, solemn orations and patriotic music in the meetinghouse. The Fourth was celebrated all across the country, of course, but it was widely believed that the most energetic, impassioned, and organized celebrations took place in New England.

Traditional Independence Day pageantry begins at the Village as the flag is raised to the ringing of bells, musket fire, and cannon salutes. In midmorning town men and women gather at the Center Meetinghouse for the "public exercises," including an early-nineteenth-century oration (drastically shortened from its original one-hour length) and patriotic songs such as "Hail Columbia." Children often play "rounders" or other nineteenth-century games, and it is the one day of the year that visiting families picnic on the Common. Extended rounds of formal toasts, usually numbering thirteen to honor the original states, are offered to patriotic themes. Afterward, a long procession of townspeople forms up near the Common behind a fife-and-drum company, flag bearers, and a militia escort. Distinguished citizens in formal clothes (only men marched in the 1830s) are followed by groups of farmers, mechanics, and scholars from the District

Above: On the Fourth of July, town officials in the dress of the 1830s gather with a uniformed veteran of the Revolutionary War—a conflict already part of the heroic past

Opposite: This decorative ribbon of 1832 marked the one-hundredth anniversary of the first president's birth—a day that continued to be an important occasion of celebration in New England

School. To the beat of the drums, they parade through the Village, taking the roads in a great loop. They return to a flag-bedecked platform in front of the Meetinghouse for an impassioned reading of the Declaration of Independence. Later in the afternoon, miniature hot-air balloons are sometimes launched, and dancers perform to the accompaniment of fiddle tunes. In many towns of the 1830s, bells and cannons brought the day to a close, with fireworks and more music to follow. A gala ball was often held in the evening to crown the celebration.

During the 1830s, Fourth of July ceremonies sometimes represented the united spirit of the community, but were just as often used to promote political parties and candidates or to trumpet reform causes. In presidential election years in particular, rival party caucuses organized elaborate competing celebrations for Whigs and Democrats. Making vivid the political disputes of the past, the Village may pit costumed supporters of the Democrats Andrew Jackson and Martin Van Buren against the Whig adherents of Daniel Webster, Henry Clay, and William Henry Harrison. The numerous reform causes of the 1830s often found voice on the Fourth as well: there were Sabbath School celebrations when schoolchildren marched, temperance festivals that brought crowds together for cold water toasts, and more controversial antislavery Fourths with fiery denunciations of slaveholders and patriotic tunes set to abolitionist words. There were historical Fourths of July as well, celebrations set aside to honor a town's hundredth (or even two-hundredth) anniversary, or to commemorate general New England anniversaries such as the landing of the Pilgrim Fathers or the arrival of the Great Fleet in Massachusetts Bay. This growing diversity of celebrations disclosed the issues and concerns of an increasingly complex society, but in every community Independence Day remained a powerful festival of national identity.

Examples from the village's remarkable
collection of early-nineteenth-century
militia uniforms and equipment

Training Days

Training days for each town's militia company were unofficial public holidays during the early nineteenth century. Under state laws, the majority of men between the ages of eighteen and forty-five were obliged to serve, equipping themselves and reporting when called for drill and inspection. Local companies trained at least twice a year, in the spring and fall, with other trainings at the option of commanders. While there were "volunteer" units in the larger towns that prided themselves on meticulous uniforms and soldierly drill, the majority were "enrolled" companies whose somewhat reluctant members earned their reputations as "ragtags" or "barnyard" militiamen. When called out for training day, the enrolled company at Old Sturbridge Village musters about twenty men in varying degrees of military dress, some with up-to-date weapons and others carrying sticks or hayforks as substitutes. The fife-and-drum players parade, and a serious and soldierly captain—in his splendid blue-and-silver officer's coatee—leads his citizen-soldiers

Opposite: *Militiamen on the Common in front of the Fitch House—a view from the Parsonage*

Below: *During the Agricultural Fair, the Center Meetinghouse becomes an exhibition hall where the most prized products of rural households, gardens, shops, and even factories are displayed*

through the evolutions prescribed by act of Congress. Maneuvers include close-order marching drill, the "rapid" loading and firing of black powder muskets in formation, and a mock attack upon the Powder House on the hill behind the Meetinghouse, where town militias stored their munitions. At times, the "sham battle" involves other re-created military units of the early nineteenth century that have been invited for the occasion. Outside the Tavern during the noon hour, the troops assemble to eat, drink toasts, demonstrate gambling and other games of the period, and talk with visitors. It is a noisy, exciting day for the entire Village, and it follows closely the many colorful accounts of such musters in the 1830s—when the hometown militias were frequently teased for their motley appearance and quixotic performance.

Agricultural Fairs

The Agricultural Fair held each September at the Village is a re-creation of a "Cattle Show, Exhibition of Manufactures, and Ploughing Match" from the 1830s. These events were a new phenomenon in the early nineteenth century, as progressively minded New England farmers established county agricultural societies and began to sponsor exhibitions that would popularize agricultural reform. At first, cattle shows were held only

at the county level, but by the 1830s annual exhibitions were being organized in smaller communities as well. As in the past, a parade of working oxen usually opens the day at Old Sturbridge Village, and premiums, or prizes, are offered for livestock on display. Temporary pens are constructed on the Common for showing oxen, heifers, and milk cows, as well as smaller numbers of pigs, sheep, and horses.

Meetinghouses or town halls were given over to the display of garden vegetables, fruits, butter, and cheese, along with home-produced goods like frocking, counterpanes, carpeting, socks, and fancy needlework. In order to link farming to rural industry, local factory and shop manufactures, such as cotton or woolen textiles, shoes, and edge tools, were often exhibited. The Village's Agricultural Fair re-creates this rich profusion. Historic flowers and vegetable varieties grown in its farms and gardens are displayed, along with heirloom plants offered by the museum's own members. There are also bonnets, tinware, quilts, and iron products chosen from the reproductions fashioned in the Village's shops and households throughout the year.

*Opposite: Farmers and their teams com-
pete in the Plowing Match at the
Agricultural Fair*

The most crowd-pleasing activities of this Agricultural Fair, as of countless others in the past, are the competitions that match men and teams against each other—plowing matches and trials of oxen. Onlookers line the fences as Village farmers and teams,
along with traditional ox teamsters invited from all over New England, match their skills
at plowing the traditional eighth of an acre. Trials of working oxen send yoked teams
through a series of challenging maneuvers while they pull a cart weighted with two tons
of stone. Throughout the day, visitors join costumed "spectators" to inspect the livestock
on the Common or examine the goods on exhibit at the Center Meetinghouse. They can
eavesdrop on the costumed judging committees at work among the exhibits, linger in
conversation with farmers, and await the yearly address on the advancement of farming
and the much-anticipated presentation of premiums.

Good Works

The impulse to reform the arrangements of society through voluntary action was nowhere
stronger in early-nineteenth-century America than in rural New England. Missionary
societies, charitable societies, lyceums that sponsored debates and lectures, and even antislavery and peace societies were founded by the hundreds. Village interpreters re-create
some of the social ferment of the 1830s with lyceum lectures, antislavery debates, missionary appeals, and the activities of women's charitable societies. On a day emphasizing the role of women in American history visitors may happen on a Charitable Society
Fair, where handmade items, refreshments, and baked goods would have been sold to
raise money for local good works, while a "Post Office" sells fanciful letters to men in the
crowd, games are offered, and "fortunes" are read. Visitors to the Fair discover that mem-
bership in the Charitable Society included the wives and daughters of ministers,
lawyers, merchants, and successful farmers and mechanics. Without the vote or any formal role in town government, these women helped the needy in ways that went beyond
poor relief and established a distinctive and influential presence for themselves in community affairs.

Dramatic lyceum presentations at the Village have reenacted debates about the
proper role of the Supreme Court, the morality of dancing, and the evils of slavery. From
time to time, the Meetinghouse and other locations in the village resound with the impassioned arguments of early New England orators and reformers. Debaters may argue
whether or not Texas should be annexed, a highly controversial topic in the 1830s, or a
speaker representing the peace movement might object to the fanfare of the militia's training day. All the reform movements of the 1830s, from antislavery and temperance to
prison reform and the earliest stirrings of feminism, brought forth divisive emotions and
excited much public controversy in New England communities. Although the brightest
hopes of the age of reform did not always come true, and some causes even dwindled
away, many of New England's famous "isms" became powerful instruments for shaping
the nation's future.

CHAPTER EIGHT

A Museum of Everyday Life

Above: At a living museum even the farm animals are historical artifacts

Opposite: In 1941 Old Sturbridge Village founders A.B. Wells (center right) and J. Cheney Wells (center left) discussed plans for the museum at the Miner Grant Store with their brother Channing Wells (left) and noted landscape architect Arthur Shurcliff (right)

THE PASSIONATE COLLECTING THAT created Old Sturbridge Village began in the 1920s. Its most decisive moment came on a rainy New Hampshire day in 1926 when Albert B. Wells, unable to play golf with friends, went on an antique-hunting expedition instead. He had done some looking and acquiring before, but that afternoon he became "hooked" on the ordinary objects of the New England past in all their variety—"my primitives," as he often called them. They included wooden bowls and country chairs, scythes and hay rakes, redware pots and butter churns; everything that bore the stamp of the countryside, of handcraftsmanship, and of ingenious contrivance was liable to be swept up in his enthusiastic acquisition. "A.B." Wells was one of the senior executives and major shareholders of the American Optical Company in Southbridge, Massachusetts; as collecting became his consuming passion, he fit it into the busy life of a prominent industrialist. His brother, Joel Cheney Wells, was likewise an American Optical executive and a significant collector in his own right. His major interest, matching his precise and methodical temperament, was in early clocks and timepieces, many of which came to adorn the company offices.

In collecting, and ultimately creating a museum, both men were following a path also trod by members of the Rockefeller, Du Pont, Ford, and other prominent American families. Heirs to industrial success, and active shapers of a high-technology industry, the brothers were fascinated with, and ultimately committed to preserving, the handmade world of the past.

As A.B.'s collection grew, it came to occupy more and more of his large

Southbridge home, first necessitating the addition of extra rooms and eventually crowding out the family completely. During the late 1920s and early 1930s a number of Wells family employees worked on sorting and arranging the collection as it grew to occupy forty-five rooms.

By 1935 the question of what to do with this extraordinary profusion of ordinary things was unavoidable. Clearly they needed to be shared with the public. That year a nonprofit educational corporation, the Wells Historical Museum, was incorporated to take ownership and display them. In July of 1936 there was a meeting of the museum's trustees—really a Wells family council—to determine what steps should be taken next. A.B. remembered that he began the meeting by proposing that several representative early New England buildings be brought to the Southbridge site, arranged in a horseshoe shape, and used as display galleries for his collections. But this plan was "knocked . . . full of holes" by his son George B. Wells, also an American Optical offi-

A mid-1930s view of a room in the Wells Historical Museum. Its densely packed, but painstakingly arranged, display echoes A.B. Wells's style as a collector

cial, who had a different conception. "He pointed out," his father recalled, "that the historical value of the things I'd been collecting was tremendous, provided that it could be put to proper usage. . . . He suggested that to make this material valuable it would be necessary to have a village, a live village, one with different shops operating . . . it was essential to have water power." George had proposed "a revolutionary idea," one that took his father and uncle off their feet but also quickly won their assent. Cheney Wells offered to add his clocks and other collections to A.B.'s and to help "in every way I can to develop a village along the lines that George suggests."

Within a few weeks, the 153-acre Wight farm in the adjoining town of Sturbridge had been purchased, complete with sloping meadows, wooded hillsides, and an excellent location for waterpower along the Quinebaug River. Site development work for the "live village" got under way, and a couple of months later the museum's first curator was hired to begin the formidable task of classifying and cataloguing a collection already numbering in the tens of thousands. With a comfortable offhandedness characteristic of the Village's early days, the Wellses acquired old New England buildings, moved them to the Village site from their original locations, and restored them. They also created new service and demonstration structures, sometimes in part out of recycled early materials, that were "sympathetic" to the design of their historical companions.

To encompass these purposes, a new organization, first called the Quinabaug Village Corporation, was chartered "to establish, maintain, and operate a model village wherein shall be exhibited and carried on for the educational benefit of the public specimens and reproductions of New England architecture and antiquities, the arts, crafts, trades, and callings commonly practiced in and about New England villages prior to the period of industrial expansion in New England."

World War II slowed, and then virtually halted, the development of the museum, as the Wellses turned their full attention to war work. With the conflict's end, the family returned to its project and made rapid progress. By 1946 the public name of the Quinabaug Village Corporation had become Old Sturbridge Village, and on June 8, the museum opened to the public under the direction of Ruth Dyer Wells, George Wells's wife and A.B.'s daughter-in-law. The staff—of office and support personnel and "hosts and hostesses"—numbered twenty-five. Around the Village's common and along its roads in 1946 were buildings still familiar to village visitors: the Miner Grant Store, the Richardson House (now the Parsonage), and the Fitch House. The Tavern was under construction as a "sympathetic" service building, and the Gristmill was running down at the Millpond. A schoolhouse and nonoperating sawmill were on display, along with many "shop" buildings that displayed and celebrated the products of early craftsmanship. Many of these structures formed an enduring nucleus for the museum; others have since been removed or given new uses as restoration and exhibit philosophy have changed. Serving to a large extent as exhibit galleries, the early buildings provided abundant displays of the collections—farming implements, shoemaking tools, woodenware, pottery, glass, toys, ironware and tinware, looms and spinning wheels, stoves, vehicles, and optical equipment. These initial accomplishments were truly impressive, but few of the 5,170 people who visited the Village that first season would have predicted its remarkable development over the next five decades.

An aerial view of Old Sturbridge
Village and its surroundings, c. 1948.
Although most of the Village's land-
mark buildings are yet to arrive, the
Meetinghouse, Richardson House,
Fitch House, Tavern, and Gristmill
can be seen

As they developed their sense of what Old Sturbridge Village should be, the Wells family stayed close to the look and feel of the New England countryside that they knew and remembered. They considered and then rejected a proposal for the creation of elegant, formal, and brick-clad structures around the Common offered by a distinguished architectural firm that had consulted with the Rockefellers on Colonial Williamsburg. Defined by craftsmen busy at their tasks, unpaved country roads, and clapboarded country buildings, the Village would be as close to the real thing as possible.

The first fifteen years were ones of very rapid growth from these modest beginnings—in visitation, in the number of buildings brought to the site and new exhibits opened, in staff, and in the variety of programs offered to the public. Craftsmanship was always a very important focus. At first the Village attempted to showcase modern-day artisans; then it began to concentrate strictly on the demonstration of historical crafts. The Village moved to full-time professional management a couple of years later, and then developed staff specialties for collections, research, education, and publications. Houses came to be furnished as historical residences. New exhibit buildings included many of the Village's now-familiar "landmarks": the Center Meetinghouse, the Pliny Freeman Farmhouse, the Printing Office, the Friends' Meetinghouse, the Fenno House, and the Salem Towne House, giving the museum the overall shape that it retains today.

The Center Meetinghouse on its original site in Fiskdale, Massachusetts, in 1948. It is being disassembled for removal to Old Sturbridge Village

Below: The Museum Education Building—a unique environment for active, participatory learning about history

Overleaf: The Asa Knight Store (left) on its original site in Dummerston, Vermont

In 1955, the nine-year-old Village and its people faced a challenge—the near-disastrous hurricane of that year, the worst in decades—that would test their resilience and determination to the utmost. Overcoming the damage done by wind and flood required herculean efforts. A high-water mark on the Gristmill memorializes the floodwaters, and a few veteran Villagers can still remember the sight of the Freeman House floating in the millpond! By the tenth anniversary the surging waters were becoming only a vivid memory.

By the end of the 1950s museum attendance had reached 250,000—a fiftyfold increase—and another major milestone was marked in 1959 when George B. Wells stepped down as president of the Board of Trustees, to be replaced by Henry S. Woodbridge, the first individual outside the Wells family to serve in that position. For the Wells family, who would continue their strong support of the Village, this change signaled a new phase of their stewardship, a welcome sharing of responsibility for the museum with the wider world. The Village was becoming an institution of national sig-

nificance with a broad base of support among those who cared about American history and New England's heritage.

In the 1960s attendance continued to grow, and the Village continued to see the professionalization of its staff and the expansion of office, library, and collections storage facilities to support the work of the museum. Acquisition of the 1,046-acre Morgan Tract dramatically expanded the Village's site, protecting the museum from commercial expansion and providing the opportunity for long-term development. Music and dramatic programs, expanded school services, and highly popular "Crafts at Close Range" workshops were developed to meet the needs of an expanding audience.

Museum standards for restoration and documentation became increasingly more rigorous with the arrival of new, exactingly researched exhibits that included the Carding Mill, the Bank, the District School, the Pottery, the Law Office, and the Cooper Shop.

Toward the end of the decade, the Village began a pathbreaking project—transforming the Pliny Freeman House and its surroundings, in a series of stages, into a genuine working farm of the early nineteenth century. Museum historians researched and re-created the routines and tools of early farmwork and reproduced early-nineteenth-century crop and livestock varieties after a painstaking search for surviving or similar modern examples. Old Sturbridge Village quickly became a national leader in "historical agriculture" and the living interpretation of history—a striking reaffirmation of the founders' conception of a "live village."

The 1970s saw both new exhibits and the rapid expansion of educational and interpretive programs. As historians of early America turned their attention to the study of work, family, and community, the Village was seen, even more than before, as a powerful resource for learning about the past. In this decade the 1830s were defined as the museum's interpretive focus, a way of synchronizing all the details of costume, furnishing, and narrative explanation so that visitors could have a seamless experience of life in an early New England community. Setting the standard for future projects was the restoration and furnishing of the Asa Knight Store from Dummerston, Vermont; its accurate and innovative reproduction of virtually the entire stock of an 1830s country store set standards widely adopted elsewhere.

Equally dramatic advances were visible in education. The Village greatly expanded the range and depth of programs offered to the schools and became a nationwide model for training teachers in the use of historical resources. By 1974 these activities were taking place in a new and strikingly innovative Museum Education Building—built in a campaign started off by a challenge gift from the Wells family—in which both children and adults could have "hands-on" experience of the past, ranging from fireplace cooking and early-nineteenth-century school lessons to working with early woodworking and farming tools.

Interpretation and demonstration underwent a comparable season of innovation and professionalization, including a greatly expanded and upgraded program of historical costume based on the museum's extraordinary collection of period clothing. Along with this went an increased emphasis on the performing and teaching roles of the Village's costumed staff. In 1975, as part of the same Wells-inspired building campaign, the new Visitor Center opened to provide a more effective front door for the Village, with facilities for admissions, orientation, meetings, performances, and gallery exhibits.

Through the 1970s and 1980s the museum expanded the range and scope of its portrayal of everyday life in the past, moving to increase both authenticity and visitor engagement. The Center Village and the Mill Neighborhood were established as distinctive exhibit areas within the historical environment. Working outbuildings—sheep sheds, horse sheds, woodsheds, barns, privies—became part of the museum landscape, along with a working horse-powered Cider Mill and a reproduction pottery kiln whose two-day-long firings became times of high drama. Shoemaking, tin manufacture, basketmaking, straw braiding, bookbinding, sewing and embroidery, construction, and bonnet making were established as working historical crafts. A re-created working Sawmill of the 1830s was built on the Millpond, after years of meticulous archaeological and technical research. Households took on new, carefully researched furnishings and social identities. The Bixby House, originally of Barre, Massachusetts, opened in 1988 as the Village's first new house exhibit in thirty years. Telling the story of an ordinary family touched by social and economic transformation, it won national recognition for its research and restoration.

Appropriately memorializing a Village founder, the J. Cheney Wells Clock Gallery was completed in 1982; it provided a climate-controlled and elegant space for the presentation of one of the museum's premier and most popular collections.

Building on the Wells collecting legacy, Old Sturbridge Village has assembled over five decades a deep, rich, and virtually unique collection, numbering nearly one hun-

dred thousand artifacts, of the objects made and used in ordinary life. They range from country furniture, rural portraits, clothing, and quilts to clocks, lighting devices, glassware, firearms, and militia equipment. Collecting to support museum programs, its Research Library has built a remarkably powerful and focused collection of printed and manuscript sources on rural New England.

With these resources, along with its living collections of historical livestock and plants and its over forty historic structures, the Village is a center for the historical, material, and archaeological study of the early American past in all its detail and specificity. Village scholars have won prizes for their work, and the museum has participated in many ways in the broader world of scholarship—all the while remaining mindful that the Village's visitors are the ultimate audience.

Greatly changed in so many ways—expanded and refined, reaching nearly half a million visitors in 1996 compared to the five thousand of 1946 and facing an uncertain new century rather than the surging postwar decades—would the Village be recognizable to its founders? The answer is surely yes. It has kept faith with their vision of a "live village," with their deep concern for hand skills and artisanship, with their abiding love of the wonderful and beautiful things of ordinary life, and with their conviction that the life of the early New England countryside is of enduring importance to our collective memory.

ACKNOWLEDGMENTS

THIS BOOK, LIKE ANY OTHER EFFORT SUPPORTED BY OLD STURBRIDGE Village, is the result of an extensive collaboration of talents and a generous sharing of resources. I learned about the intricate, changing patterns of New England country life from museum researchers and my fellow interpreters during the nine years that I worked at the Village. Now, some five years later, my writing for this project has been mainly a process of summarizing and collating their fascinating discoveries and allowing their work to inform every line of the account.

The idea for the book was encouraged from the outset by the President of Old Sturbridge Village, Alberta Sebolt George; and many other former colleagues at the Village made indispensable contributions to the many aspects of its production. Finally, Eric Himmel, Rachel Tsutsumi, and Dirk Luykx at Harry N. Abrams, Inc., helped to tie all the disparate threads together.

Index

Note: Page numbers in *italics* refer to illustrations. Captions are indexed as text.